RadioWaves

The Health Edition

Mary Lee Wholey
Judith Ritter

HEINLE & HEINLE PUBLISHERS

I(T)P An International Thomson Publishing Company
Boston, Massachusetts 02116 USA

New York • London • Bonn • Boston • Detroit • Madrid • Melbourne • Mexico City
Paris • Singapore • Tokyo • Toronto • Washington • Albany NY • Belmont CA • Cincinnati OH

The publication of *RadioWaves: The Health Edition* was directed by the members of the Global Innovations Publishing Team at Heinle & Heinle:

David C. Lee, Editorial Director
John F. McHugh, Market Development Director
Martha M. Liebs, Production Editor
Also participating in the publication of this program were:
Publisher: Stanley J. Galek
Editorial Production Manager: Elizabeth Holthaus
Project Manager: Publication Services
Assistant Editor: Kenneth Mattsson
Production Assistant: Maryellen Eschmann
Manufacturing Coordinator: Mary Beth Hennebury
Cover Illustrator: Dana Knight Communications
Cover Designer: Dana Knight Communications

Copyright © 1995
by Heinle & Heinle Publishers
An International Thomson Publishing Company

All rights reserved. No part of this publication may be reproduced or transmitted in any form or by any means, electronic or mechanical, including photocopy, recording, or any information storage and retrieval system, without permission in writing from the publisher.

Manufactured in the United States of America
ISBN: 0-8384 5795-9

10 9 8 7 6 5 4 3 2 1

Table of Contents

PREFACE	v
NOTES TO THE TEACHER	vii
NOTES TO THE INDIVIDUAL USER	ix
ACKNOWLEDGMENTS	x
OVERVIEW	xi
UNIT 1: MEDICAL EMERGENCY 911	**1**
Preparing to Listen	2
Listening to the Tape	5
Language Close Up	10
Follow-Up	12
UNIT 2: BUTTING OUT IN THE BOARD ROOM	**21**
Preparing to Listen	22
Listening to the Tape	25
Language Close Up	29
Follow-Up	32
UNIT 3: SUMMER CAMP FOR SICK KIDS	**39**
Preparing to Listen	40
Listening to the Tape	42
Language Close Up	46
Follow-Up	48
UNIT 4: TINY SURVIVORS: SAVING PREEMIES	**55**
Preparing to Listen	56
Listening to the Tape	59
Language Close Up	63
Follow-Up	66
UNIT 5: TOP DOGS IN DETROIT: EYES FOR THE UNSIGHTED	**75**
Preparing to Listen	76
Listening to the Tape	81
Language Close Up	84
Follow-Up	86
APPENDIX 1: GUIDE TO NOTE TAKING	**93**
APPENDIX 2: REPORTERS' BIOGRAPHIES AND TRANSCRIPTS	**100**
APPENDIX 3: ANSWER KEY	**108**

All Reviewers and Consultants for Radiowaves:

David Allen	Long Island University	Gary Dyck	University of Manitoba
Lida Baker	University of California, Los Angeles	Michael Feldman	Boston University
Richard Bier	Indiana University	Linda Robinson Fellag	Community College of Philadelphia
Sharon Bode	University of Pennsylvania	John Fitzer	State University of New York at Buffalo
Gerald Lee Boyd	Northern Virginia Community College	Judy Graves	Eurocenters Alexandria
Kim Brown	Portland State University	Mary Hill-Shinn	El Paso Community College
Barbara Campbell	State University of New York at Buffalo	Tom Hoffman	University of Kansas
Debra Dean	University of Akron	Helen Huntley	Ohio University
Marta Dmytrenko-Aharbian	Wayne State University	Gary James	Honolulu

PREFACE

The Programs

The *RadioWaves* series brings authentic-quality radio reports into the domain of the ESL or EFL learner. The series includes six programs: the Health Edition, the Entertainment Edition, the Business Edition, the Environment Edition, the Sports Edition, and the Music Edition. Each program features five 5-minute reports in a "newsmagazine" format. The information is presented in a style that blends journalistic and academic formats. These programs open the doors to a wealth of North American culture in a radio format that is typically American. The student will learn about current topics that are heard on radio and television, in public discussion, in academic, professional, and social situations. This series allows the learner to become more comfortable with and confident about listening to radio reports. In short, *RadioWaves* brings real-world listening and exciting ideas into the learner's realm of experience.

Language Principles

Each of the editions in the *RadioWaves* series includes a tape and a workbook. The workbook materials are based on a set of fundamental language-learning and teaching principles. These principles include the following:

1. Skills are not acquired in isolation. Listening is intimately tied to speaking, and reading and writing about what was heard help improve listening comprehension.
2. Language learning in the classroom is best facilitated by interaction. The learner should have many opportunities to exchange information with others.
3. Listening comprehension develops as the learner listens actively to complete a task. The learner has a purpose in listening and can use what has been understood.
4. A learner uses certain skills and strategies to understand what is heard. These can be identified and improved on through the undertaking of a well-designed task or series of tasks.

Skills and Strategies

RadioWaves is designed to help the learner acquire the skills and strategies needed to get more from listening. The series makes listening to and understanding radio reports easier. The skills and strategies that are used and developed are transferable to other listening context, such as formal and informal social settings and academic settings.

The principal skills developed are listening for main ideas and note taking. The series shows the learner how to find and state the main ideas in a report. The learner is guided in learning to take notes from radio reports. Some programs in the series teach the learner to recognize the organization of journalistic reports that follow an academic format. These programs present a series of main ideas and supporting points, and elaborate on each in sequence.

An approach more frequently used in this series is focused note taking. Taking focused notes involves writing supporting points and details related to a general question. The general question reflects an important point or idea the reporter chooses to focus on and develop, either through interviews or through explanations and commentary on the topic. The purpose of focused note taking is to sensitize the learner to the organization of radio reports, which can often be determined from the reporters' questions or the selection of issues for the program.

This series helps the learner to develop a number of useful strategies so that listening can be approached with more confidence. The learner needs to be shown how to carry out a number of different learning tasks. To accomplish this the learner should know which strategies to use and develop. These strategies include the following:

1. Looking for the overall structure of the information.
2. Knowing the signals used to introduce main points.
3. Knowing that main points or ideas are usually followed by information that elaborates on those ideas.
4. Knowing that information is often restated.
5. Recognizing key information (main ideas and details) and distinguishing it from unimportant information, for example, asides, personal remarks, and certain features of spoken language such as false starts or interrupters.
6. Predicting what one thinks will be heard to help recognize ideas more quickly and clearly.
7. Knowing that the process of using information to complete a task increases understanding.
8. Knowing that exchanging information with others is useful in increasing comprehension.
9. Knowing that with successive listening opportunities, a more complete understanding of the information is gradually built up.
10. Knowing that learning to guess from context and cope with uncertainty will help to increase comprehension.
11. Evaluating one's progress in understanding and using a second or foreign language.
12. Taking responsibility for one's learning and seeking out opportunities to improve.

The Task

Listening comprehension is facilitated through structuring tasks to encourage learners to engage in purposeful, active listening and use the information heard. The principal listening tasks consist of main idea identification and note-taking activities. In addition, learners answer a number of short-answer questions that focus on accuracy. A number of related activities are included before and after the principal listening tasks. These tasks help learners to prepare for the information and to build on their understanding of the topic. The tasks are integrated; learners note information as they listen because they need to use it both immediately and for later speaking, reading, or writing activities. The tasks encourage cooperation as the learners exchange ideas, confirming what was heard. They also help build independence as the learners undertake individual tasks, selecting from the information that which is of personal interest, in order to give opinions, reach conclusions, and critically evaluate what was heard. In addition, learners are encouraged to make choices about how to follow up and select tasks that suit their needs.

Each edition contains five programs of similar length and complexity. Task complexity within each unit is structured so that the learners gradually build up and refine their skills and develop useful strategies to enable them to handle the information they hear with increasing ease. To this end, the activities in the first units in each edition provide more guidance in finding main ideas and building note-taking skills than do the activities in later units.

Notes to the Teacher

The RadioWaves series is a versatile program. It can be used in a variety of settings both inside and outside the classroom.

Classroom Use

1. Whole-class listening, in which all the students hear the same program as a group. Here the pace of the listening is teacher controlled.
2. Small-group listening, in which learners listen using one machine with three or four sets of earphones per group. Here, learners have more control over the pace of their listening. With four or five small, four-plug cassette machines and earphones, you can turn your classroom into a listening center.

Listening Retells

A listening retell is an activity in which learners listen to two different programs and report on them to each other. In listening centers or in separate classrooms, members of the same class can listen to different taped programs. Learners listening to the same report work together to take notes and then use their notes to orally explain the information they heard to those who heard a different report. Setting up a listening retell situation like this creates an authentic communication activity in which the groups hear and tell about a program in much the same way they would in everyday life.

Language Labs

In traditional language labs students may have some opportunity to control their own pace of listening.

Individual Use/Self-Study

The programs can be used for individual learning at home or at a resource center with audio facilities.

Organization of the Unit

The activities of each unit in each edition are divided into four sections: Preparing to Listen, Listening to the Tape, Language Close Up, and Follow-Up

Section One: Preparing to Listen

This section serves a number of purposes. One is to give learners an opportunity to think about ideas that will be focused on in the program in order to stimulate curiosity about the topic, activate prior knowledge, and help the learners predict the content to some extent. Another purpose is to introduce learners to key ideas and important background information that will decrease their difficulty in understanding the information they hear and help them accomplish the tasks in the next section. To this end, one or two of the activities give learners a chance to read and gather information on the topic.

The "Preparing to Listen" section can be augmented and adapted to meet the needs of your group. In following the instructions for the activities, keep in mind the abilities of the learners and their familiarity with the methodology. To make the task less difficult, you can teacher-center occasionally to elicit ideas from the whole class. For example, after the prediction activity, you could teacher-center the discussion and write suggestions on the board. Similarly, at the end of the "Bridge to Listening" section, you could teacher-center the discussion, elicit the answers, and compare the information the class heard to the predictions they made. Once learners are familiar with the methodology, teacher-centering this type of activity is not necessary.

When learners are working in pairs or in groups, your role is to help individuals share the information with each other, to encourage interaction, and to help the learners keep on task. Monitor your class's activity in order to intervene when necessary to keep the pace lively. As learners progress, it may be possible to vary the task by having learners work in groups rather than in pairs, and by inviting learners to exchange information with new partners or initiate tasks of their own.

Section Two: Listening to the Tape

The activities in this section consist of listening for main ideas, listening and taking notes, and using notes to answer detailed questions.

Listening for Main Ideas

These activities are structured so that in the first programs, learners listen and put in order the ideas from a scrambled list. They only have to identify the ideas as they listen. For reports that have a more academic organization, where the main ideas are clearly signaled, and in the last report of each edition, learners listen and write the ideas on their own. Thus, there is a clear progression in the difficulty of the tasks.

The first time learners undertake this task or the first time they have to write the main ideas without aid, you can elicit the answers and write them on the board. In this way the ideas can be identified for all and you can point out how to state a main idea and how to recognize different ways of stating the same idea.

Note Taking

The note-taking activities give students practice in developing note-taking skills. In the first program of each edition, a section of essential component skills is provided. Teacher-centering the class to transmit this information is useful; you can give examples of how to abbreviate, how to use symbols and numerals, and how to paraphrase. It is important to stress that acquiring these skills takes time and practice. When learners share their information in pairs or in groups, it is a good time to give individuals feedback on the development of their note-taking skills. Again, teacher-center occasionally to show what information to write in notes and how to write it. You may ask learners to reorganize information as a homework assignment to help improve their skills. Circulate from group to group as people exchange information from their notes to make sure they are adding new information as they discuss.

Progression in note taking is built into the academic-style note-taking activities in the following way: If more than one of these activities is included in an edition, the second is usually less guided than the first. You can tailor these activities to needs of your learners.

An expanded "Guide to Note Taking" is included as the appendix in each workbook. Use it as a reference for those who want information on how to improve their skills. Gauge your learners' needs for guidance and practice in building their skills. Optional steps for note taking and answer verification are built into the activities. You may want to skip these steps or introduce an added step to give students more opportunities to listen. In addition, you can structure additional note-taking activities from material heard in the program to provide extra practice.

Comprehension Questions

Learners use their notes to answer comprehension questions and then check their answers orally in pairs. An additional listening to confirm or complete answers is suggested. You may want to use this optional step the first time learners answer, or with a group that needs more opportunities for practice. If you wish to decrease the difficulty of the listening task, learners could read the questions and listen for answers to the questions in this section before attempting the note-taking tasks. The comprehension questions can be used as an evaluation tool for individual assessment.

Section Three: Language Close Up

The activities in this section give you a choice of language focus tasks to help fine-tune listening. The activities focus on grammatical form through the completion of cloze tasks. Other activities focus on aspects of understanding spoken language, identifying signal markers, identifying and interpreting point of view, and paraphrasing information. Finally, the section includes activities that help students develop their skill at guessing the meaning of new words. Learners may work on these sections individually, at home, or in a language lab.

The activities in this section were structured to reflect important features of the language of the program and to have teachable qualities. In other words, the activities present language points that are clear and useful. Naturally, these activities do not exhaust the possibilities for learning. Learners can be directed to find other instances of the point focused on in an activity in this section, or different points that are appropriate to the focus of instruction in your course.

Section Four: Follow-Up

This section contains activities that encourage learners to expand on, select from, and use the information they heard in the program. Generally speaking, this section provides further readings on the topic. Many of the reading tasks are interactive retells that provide an opportunity for learners to use their note-taking skills in a new context to gain more oral practice. Further activities allow learners opportunities to use their language skills outside of class and to comment on the information they gather.

Notes To the Individual User

The *RadioWaves* series offers many listening opportunities. If you are using this material on your own, you can adapt the activities in a number of ways.

Preparing to Listen

Use the discussion question section to help you think about the ideas in the program. Write your answers to the questions. Complete the other activities on your own. Use the answer key to confirm your answers. When activities call for information to be gathered from two texts, answer the questions from both texts and check your answers with the answer key.

Listening to the Tape

Follow the instructions for main-idea and note-taking questions. You may listen an additional time for some of these activities in order to increase comprehension. You may want to use the comprehension question activity as a check on comprehension. Answer as many questions as possible from your notes. Check your answers with the answer key. Listen again to hear the correct information.

Language Close Up

Most of the activities in this section can be worked on individually. Check your answers with the answer key.

Follow-Up

The activities in this section will expand your knowledge of the topic. Complete the reading activities and check the answer key to confirm your answers. Work through the summary-writing activities and tape a three-minute talk to give yourself another opportunity to use the information you heard in this program.

Acknowledgments

We are grateful to David Lee, who saw the merit in this project and supported it from the beginning. Thanks also to assistant editor Ken Mattsson for his invaluable help throughout the drafting and editing of the material.

We would also like to thank the following people, who read drafts of this manuscript and who made many useful comments and suggestions.

Thanks also go to colleagues at Concordia University's Continuing Education Language Institute (CELI) for their help in the preparation of this material. We are grateful to Adrianne Sklar and Gerard Bates for testing the material in their classrooms and for their advice. A particular thanks to Anna Thibeault and Nadia Henein for their unstinting work, their comments, and their help in the preparation of these materials.

Whatever is good in these materials is due to Phyllis Vogel, Lili Ullmann, and Susan Parks, from whom so much has been learned and with whom so much was shared in the years of teaching second-language students at CELI.

Finally, a special thanks to our friends and families—especially Devorah Ritter, Jonah Wexler, Yaël Wexler and Jerry Wexler—who were so understanding and supportive during the time it took to prepare this series.

OVERVIEW OF THE HEALTH EDITION

Unit 1—Medical Emergency 911

Listening

All Activities:　　Exchange of Information in Pair or Group Work

Listening to the Tape: Main Ideas Ordering; Introduction to Note-Taking Skills

Language Focus: Descriptive Detail; Recognizing Tone of Voice; Guessing Vocabulary from Context; Defining Medical Terminology

Follow-Up: At-Home Listening Task

Speaking

All Activities:　　Discussion and Information Exchange in Pair or Group Work

Follow-Up: Interviewing Skills

Reading and Writing

Pre/Post-Reading:　　Gathering Information from Pamphlets/Reports; Reading Retells
Newsmagazine Reading; Prediction; Scanning; Close Reading; Answering Questions

Free-Writing　　Synthesizing Information; Expressing Opinion

Unit 2—Butting Out in the Board Room

Listening

All Activities:　　Exchange of Information in Pair or Group Work

Listening to the Tape: Main Ideas Selection; Note-Taking Skills; Main Ideas and Details

Language Focus: Recognizing Different Aspects of Informal Speech; Grammatical Awareness—Verbs and Verb Forms; Guessing Meaning from Context

Speaking

All Activities:　　Discussion and Information Exchange in Pair or Group Work

Follow-Up: Interviewing Skills

Reading and Writing

Pre/Post-Reading:　　Reading Charts/Graphs; Reading Retells; Previewing Texts for Main Ideas; Scanning for Information to Answer Questions

Unit 3—Summer Camp for Sick Kids

Listening

All Activities:　　Exchange of Information in Pair or Group Work

Listening to the Tape: Main Ideas Ordering; Note-Taking Skills; Focused Notes

	Language Focus: Descriptive Detail; Recognizing Types/Forms of Informal Speech; Guessing Meaning from Context

Speaking

All Activities:	Discussion and Information Exchange in Pair or Group Work
	Follow-Up: Book Talk; Discussion; Presentation Skills

Reading and Writing

Pre/Post-Reading:	Illustrated Texts; Reading Retells Newsmagazine Articles; Answering Questions
	Follow-Up: Book Reading and Report

Unit 4—Tiny Survivors: Saving Preemies

Listening

All Activities:	Exchange of Information in Pair or Group Work
	Listening to the Tape: Main Ideas Ordering; Note-Taking Skills; Focused Notes
	Language Focus: Grammatical Form; Verbs; Word Roots; Prefixes and Suffixes; Guessing Meaning from Context
	Follow-Up: At-Home Listening Task

Speaking

All Activities:	Discussion and Information Exchange in Pair or Group Work

Reading and Writing

Pre/Post-Reading:	Reading Charts; Predictions; Scanning for Information Newsmagazine Articles; Note taking; Reading Retells

Unit 5—Top Dogs in Detroit: Eyes for the Unsighted

Listening

All Activities:	Exchange of Information in Pair or Group Work
	Listening to the Tape: Main Ideas Selection; Note-Taking Skills; Focused Notes
	Language Focus: Question Form; Word Roots; Prefixes and Suffixes; Guessing Meaning from Context
	Follow-Up: At-Home Listening Task

Speaking

All Activities:	Discussion and Information Exchange in Pair or Group Work

Reading and Writing

Pre/Post-Reading:	Reading Information Pamphlets; Illustrated Texts; Reading Retells; Predictions; Scanning for Information
Self-Evaluation:	Skills and Strategies

Medical Emergency 911

OVERVIEW

Preparing to Listen

Activity One	Discussion Questions
Activity Two	Gathering Information from a Pamphlet
Activity Three	Defining Medical Terms
Activity Four	Predictions; Bridge to Listening

Listening to the Tape

Activity Five	Listening for the Main Ideas
Activity Six	Writing Focused Notes
Activity Seven	Comprehension Questions

Language Close Up

| Activity Eight | Language Focus: What Was Said? |
| Activity Nine | Vocabulary: Guessing Meaning from Context |

Follow-Up

Activity Ten	Gathering Information from Reading
Activity Eleven	Conducting Interviews
Activity Twelve	Using Your Skills at Home

If you've ever experienced a medical emergency then you know how important getting help quickly can be. This program brings you up close to look at one of the most comprehensive systems for delivering emergency care in the United States. You will hear from the people who work in this system as they explain how they work and how the system operates. The activities will help you to understand and use the information you listen to.

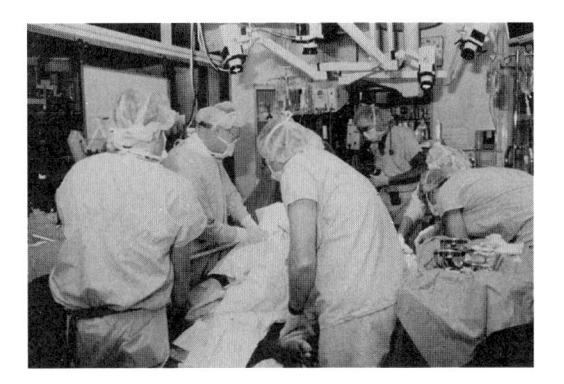

Photos courtesy of Maryland's Emergency Medical System

Preparing to Listen

Getting some background information and thinking about the topic before you hear the program will help you to understand the ideas more easily. Complete the activities in this section **before you listen.**

ACTIVITY ONE   Discussion Questions

What do you think? Read and consider the following questions. Write your ideas in note form and discuss them with others.

1. What kind of emergencies commonly occur?

2. What kind of emergency services do people need? Are the needs of urban, suburban, and rural areas different? Explain.

3. Is it necessary to have emergency services available to all people at all hours in all places? Why or why not?

4. Why are emergency systems costly? Is the cost justifiable?

5. Do emergency doctors and nurses need special training, or is the general training that most doctors and nurses have sufficient for the kinds of medical problems that they face in an emergency room?

6. Have you ever needed to use emergency services? Would you know how to summon emergency services if you needed to?

7. Where and how could people get information about emergency services or about what to do in an emergency?

ACTIVITY TWO   Gathering Information from a Pamphlet

This program focuses on the emergency system in the State of Maryland. The Maryland Institute for Emergency Medical Services has printed a pamphlet explaining the services they offer and giving advice to people involved in an emergency situation. In this activity you will gather some information from the pamphlet to answer a few key questions.

Step 1. Prediction:
Read the following questions and decide the answer you think is best for each. Write down your ideas and discuss them with others.

1. What is the most important thing to do in an emergency?

2. What should you do if you see an accident on the highway?

3. What should you do if you hear a siren or see the flashing lights of an emergency vehicle?

4. What kind of medical services and equipment are available in Maryland to handle different kinds of emergencies?

5. How fast can ambulance personnel get to the scene of an accident?

Step 2. Skim the pamphlet (read quickly for key words) and find the answers to the questions above.

Maryland's Statewide Emergency Medical Services System

Critically ill or injured patients need treatment at the hospital that is best staffed and equipped to meet their needs. Maryland's "echelons of care" ensures that patients reach the most appropriate hospital in the shortest time possible.

There are 50 hospitals with 24-hour emergency department care, 10 areawide trauma centers, and the Shock Trauma Center in Baltimore, which treats the most critically injured patients. Also included in this hospital network are 20 specialty referral centers treating patients with specialized needs, such as head trauma, spinal cord injuries, pediatric trauma, burns, eye trauma, or severe extremity injuries, as well as those needing neonatal or perinatal care. A network of ambulances and of Maryland State Police medevac helicopters capable of travelling up to 201 miles an hour stand ready to transport patients from all over the state to these hospitals.

In Maryland, however, treatment begins not at the hospital but at the scene of the emergency. More than 22,000 prehospital care providers from more than 350 volunteer and career companies work side-by-side in this state to provide professional care. Each provider receives standardized training and is state certified; this ensures a consistent level of care everywhere in the state. Each follows medical protocols and can seek physician consultation as needed.

A statewide communications system links these prehospital care providers on ambulances or helicopters with hospital-based physicians and also keeps the hospitals informed of the patient's condition while the patient is still en route to the hospital.

Maryland's emergency medical services system provides a synchronized response to injuries occurring within Maryland—regardless of time, place, or severity of injury.

If you see a motor vehicle accident, prevent further accidents.

When Seconds Count... CALL 9·1·1

UNIVERSITY OF MARYLAND
MARYLAND INSTITUTE FOR EMERGENCY MEDICAL SERVICES SYSTEMS
22 S. GREENE STREET • BALTIMORE, MD 21201-1595
July 1990

> The most important thing to do in an emergency is to call 9-1-1 for emergency medical assistance. Maryland has a sophisticated system of emergency care. Professionally trained ambulance personnel will be at the scene in a few minutes.

- Pull ahead and completely off the road. Put on emergency flashers.
- Before you call for help, try to determine where you are on the highway. Look for a mile marker, exit sign, or some other identifying feature to guide rescuers.
- Send someone to get aid or use Channel 9 on your CB radio to call for help.
- Cellular phones can be used to access the 9-1-1 system free of charge. (Check with your cellular service company for details.)
- Give the accident location, type of accident, number of victims, and your name.
- Do not move victims unless there is danger of fire, explosion, or further injures.
- Nearby hospitals are marked by a blue highway sign with a large white H on it.

How similar were the answers you found in the pamphlet to the answers you predicted in Step 1?

Step 3. Discuss your answers with a partner or check the answer key.

ACTIVITY THREE

Defining Medical Terms

In this program you will hear people describe medical situations: the problems, the equipment, and the treatment given by trained personnel in life and death situations.

Read this list of medical terms and match each term in Column A with the explanation in Column B that fits it best.

Column A	Column B
1. He is a **paramedic**.	A. A blood product that is given when a patient has lost blood.
2. He took the man's **blood pressure**.	B. A trained emergency medical worker.
3. The man needed to receive **blood plasma**.	C. A helicopter that is specially equipped to transport emergency patients to hospital.
4. He gave the medication through an **intravenous needle**.	D. The force of blood on the walls of blood vessels as it flows through the body's circulatory system.
5. They used a **med-evac helicopter** to transport the patient quickly.	E. A needle connected to tubes inserted under the skin into a vein to bring medication directly into the bloodstream.

ACTIVITY FOUR

Predictions; Bridge to Listening

Discuss your answers or check the answer key.

Part One: Predictions

Based on what you have thought about and discussed so far, make a few predictions about the ideas you expect to find out about in this program.

Write your ideas on the lines below. You can write your ideas in either words or phrases, in question or sentence form. Write any ideas you have. Don't worry about whether they are good or bad, or whether they are correctly written.

Two predictions are given as examples to help you get started.

1. How fast an ambulance can get to an accident.
2. How good this system is; how it works.
3. _____
4. _____
5. _____

Discuss your predictions. Later, you can check to see what you were able to predict.

Part Two: Bridge to Listening

The purpose of the introduction is to prepare you for the information in the program. It will give you an overview or a taste of something interesting to come.

Step 1. Cue your tape to the introduction of the show, which begins, "Maryland may be a small state." Turn on the tape.

Step 2. Listen to the introduction, which ends, "on a tour of Maryland's Quick Response Emergency System," without stopping the tape. Think about the information as you listen. Stop the tape at the end of the introduction.

Step 3. From what you recall, answer as many questions as possible in note form. The first answer is given as an example.

1. What state's emergency medical system is explained in this program and why?

    Maryland - major player - emergency med. services

2. How many hospitals are part of this system?

3. How many hospitals have shock trauma units?

4. What is the function of the communications center?

Step 4. Discuss your ideas with a partner or check the answer key. Compare these ideas to the predictions you made before.

Listening to the Tape

The activities in this section will help you to practice your skills in understanding and using the information you hear. Concentrate on the task you have to accomplish and practice the skills, such as note taking or listening for details, needed to complete the task.

> **STRATEGIES FOR COPING/NOTING INFORMATION FROM LISTENING**
>
> 1. Focus on the information you understand; don't worry about what you miss.
> 2. Remember that all listeners lose a certain percentage of any information they listen to for a number of different reasons.
> 3. If you are working with others, discuss the information to help clarify ideas when you're not sure of what you heard or you need more information.

> 4. If you are working alone, get as much information as you can.
> 5. You can listen again to get important information you may have missed.

Note Taking

In many of the activities that follow, you will be identifying the main ideas, supporting points, and details and often writing what you hear in note form. These activities will help you get more of the important information in your notes more quickly. Here are a few tips about writing quick notes as you listen:

Use Key Words, Symbols, and Abbreviations

- Write only the important words and key phrases—not whole sentences.
- Use abbreviations for words when possible.
  - Example: Abbreviate "emergency system" by writing *em. sys.*, or use *p.med.* for the word "paramedic."
  - For nonstandard abbreviations like these, always write the complete word the first time with the abbr. beside it, so that you won't forget the meaning. There are standard abbreviations such as *MD* for "Maryland" and *N.B.* for "important to remember."
- Use numerals, *911* for example, instead of writing *nine-one-one*.
- Use symbols like = to show that ideas are the same or equally important.

Spacing

- Use spacing to show important relationships of groups of words.
- Write separate words on a separate line and indent. Indenting details shows that the details pertain to a particular idea.
  - Example:
    Questions for Emergency
    -What kind of help
    -Where's the closest hosp.

Paraphrasing

- Paraphrase the information you hear when you write your notes.
- Paraphrasing involves choosing a word of your own that summarizes the ideas you hear.
  - Example: Use the word "fast" to express the idea "with the least delay."
- Remember: When you paraphrase, the word you write in your notes conveys **the same meaning** as the information you heard.

Remember that there are differences in the ways individuals take notes. The examples that are given show **one** way to note information. You will develop and improve your own style of note taking as you complete the activities in this section.

For more information about improving your note-taking skill, refer to the Guide to Note Taking (Appendix 1, p. 93).

ACTIVITY FIVE — Listening for the Main Ideas

DIRECTIONS

Step 1. Listen to the program "Medical Emergency 911" without stopping. Number the following main ideas according to the order in which you hear them.

( ) **A.** Treatment by ambulance workers
( ) **B.** Response to shooting accident
( ) **C.** Purpose of SYSCOM
( ) **D.** How SYSCOM (system communications) operates

Step 2. Discuss your answers with a partner or check the answer key.

ACTIVITY SIX — Writing Focused Notes

When you listen to a radio report, you hear a wonderful mix of voices and sounds. The information that you hear is a mixture of factual information blended with opinion and emotion. A radio report isn't always organized in the same logical pattern as a good academic lecture. It follows a pattern of describing or explaining the important ideas (main points and details) related to the topic from the reporter's point of view.

Your task is to listen and take notes so that you will be able to explain the main points and important details of this report to someone who has questions about Maryland's emergency system. The focused notes you write for the general questions will help you to discuss the details of what you heard with others.

DIRECTIONS To take focused notes follow these steps:

Step 1. Read the following general questions and think about the information you heard. What details relating to each question can you recall?

1. What happens in Maryland when there is a serious accident?
2. What response is made to the accident reported to 911? What does Lieutenant Mike Fahey do?
3. What do the ambulance paramedics do for this patient?
4. What is SYSCOM? What does it do?
5. What is the purpose of this system?

Step 2. If possible, discuss these questions with others.

Step 3. Rewind to the beginning of the program and listen a second time. Start the tape and, as you listen, write details in note form for each of the questions you have just read and discussed.

Read the sample notes to see what kind of detail is important and how to write in note form. Try taking notes yourself as you listen to the tape. Compare what you have written to the sample notes provided. Your wording may not be the same, but the ideas should be.

1. What happens in Maryland when there is a serious accident?

    H. staff/P. meds/others
    Comm. Sys.
    Where/When/Acc.

> Immed. care—Save life
> Dr. M./Trauma:
>   Right treat./Least delay/Anywhere
> Questions:
>   Help?
>   Closest hospital?
>   Amb./heli.?
> Answer: Comm. 911
> Fire Dept. Emer. Rescue
> Radio call

2. What response is made to the accident reported to 911? What does Lieutenant Mike Fahey do?

3. What do the ambulance paramedics do for this patient?

4. What is SYSCOM? What does it do?

5. What is the purpose of this system?

Step 4. Stop the tape at the end of the program and read over your notes. If you have a partner, discuss what you heard and wrote. As you read and discuss, add information to your notes.

Step 5 (Optional). Listen another time to confirm and complete your notes. Read your notes or discuss again.

ACTIVITY SEVEN   Comprehension Questions

Answering these questions correctly is a check on the accuracy of your listening.

Step 1. Read the following questions. Use your notes to answer as many as possible. Write the answers to these questions **in note form.** The first question is done by way of example.

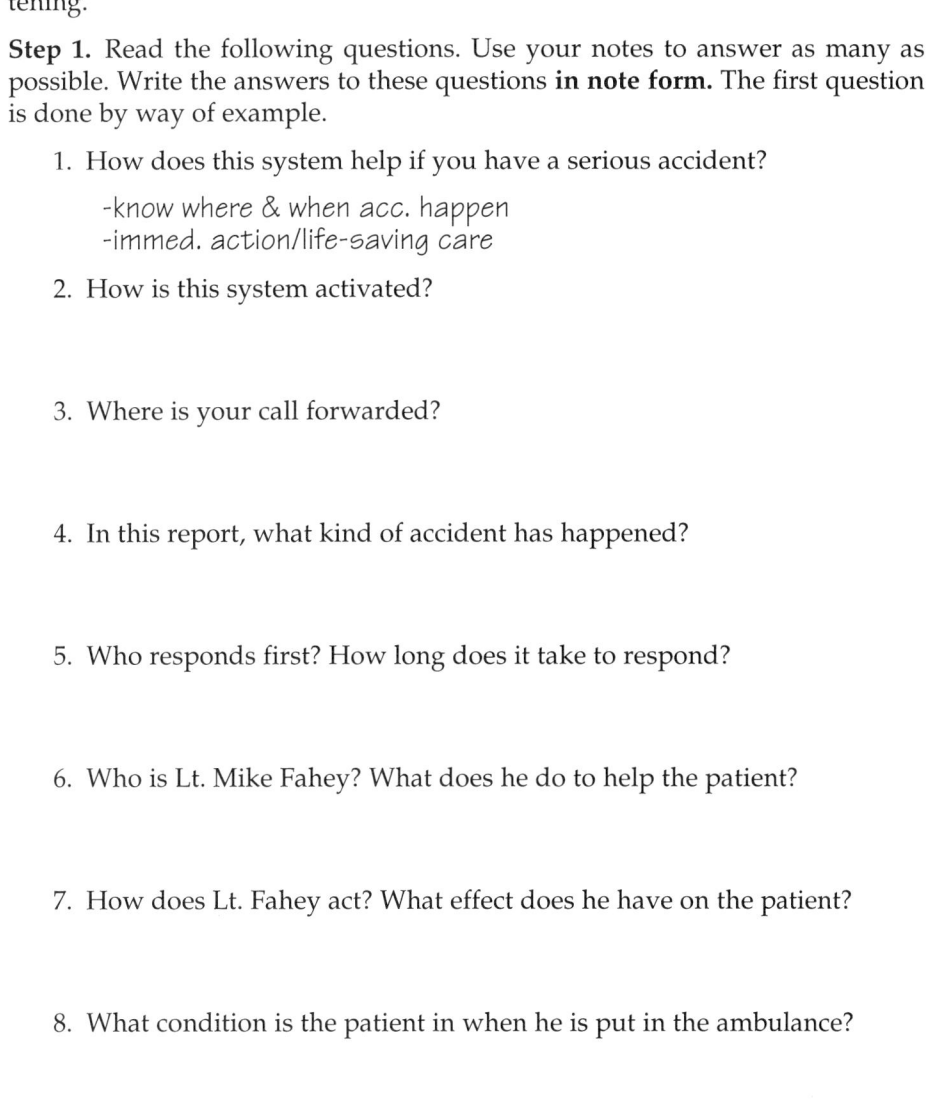

1. How does this system help if you have a serious accident?

    -know where & when acc. happen
    -immed. action/life-saving care

2. How is this system activated?

3. Where is your call forwarded?

4. In this report, what kind of accident has happened?

5. Who responds first? How long does it take to respond?

6. Who is Lt. Mike Fahey? What does he do to help the patient?

7. How does Lt. Fahey act? What effect does he have on the patient?

8. What condition is the patient in when he is put in the ambulance?

9. Inside the ambulance, what does the team do to help the patient?

10. What has everyone agreed to do for this man? Why?

11. How do they decide between taking a patient by land or by air?

12. What is SYSCOM? What does the control room consist of?

13. What important function does SYSCOM serve?

14. What can SYSCOM do for paramedics?

15. According to Dr. R. Adams Cowley, what needs to be done in order to save a person's life?

Step 2. Discuss the information with others.

Step 3 (Optional). If you need to, listen to the program to find answers that you don't have or can't agree on. Stop the tape when you hear the information you are listening for and write your answer.

Language Close Up

In this section you can practice listening for specific language. The activities focus on different features, such as improving your awareness of grammatical form or improving your ability to hear key details. The activities will help you to be more aware of the different tones, colloquial expressions, and speaking styles people use when they talk. You can learn vocabulary through the practice of guessing meaning from context.

ACTIVITY EIGHT

Language Focus: What Was Said?

In this program a number of people talk about the work they do and the importance of that work. In addition to the words they use, their tone of voice gives you information about how they feel about this work.

Listen to the following quotations from interviews in the program and identify the speaker, the job that person does, and, if possible, the person's attitude toward their job.

Cue the tape to the beginning of each quote. Listen to the entire quote. Stop the tape at the end of the quotation to give yourself time to write.

1. Serious accident happens . . . summoned immediately to provide the initial quick life-saving care.

   Speaker: _____

   Job: _____

   Attitude toward job: _____

2. Come in, take control of the situation, remain calm . . . then they calm down.

   Speaker: _____

   Job: _____

   Attitude toward job: _____

3. If we can get the patient to the trauma center . . . try to go by air.

   Speaker: _____

   Job: _____

   Attitude toward job: _____

4. Part of the operation here is the SYSCOM operation, . . . and the U.S. Park Police headquarters.

   Speaker: _____

   Job: _____

   Attitude toward job: _____

Listen again or check the answer key. With a partner, discuss your answers about the speakers' attitudes toward their jobs. Compare the similarities and differences in your answers and the reasons for your choices.

ACTIVITY NINE   Vocabulary: Guessing Meaning from Context

You have heard the words **in bold print** in the program. In this activity you will focus on the language used and guess the meaning of these words from the context in which they are used.

Step 1. Read each sentence. Based on your understanding of the sentence, try to guess what the word or words mean.

Step 2. Write your own definition for the words in bold print. You can check your definition with a partner or consult your dictionary.

1. She wanted us to call for medical help, so we **summoned** our next-door neighbor, who is a nurse, to come over to our house.

   Definition: _____

2. The fire department doesn't waste time; they **spring into action** and get to work as soon as they arrive.

   Definition: _____

3. I have to go out of town for a few days, so I've arranged for my phone calls to be **forwarded** to the place where I will be so that I won't miss your call.

   Definition: _____

4. The **dispatch** office will send you all your messages.

   Definition: _____

5. How many times do I have to tell you to sit up straight; don't **slump** in your chair.

   Definition: _____

6. The weather had been hot all week; by the weekend thousands of people were **swarming** to the beach.

   Definition: _____

7. The excitement of hearing the band was **contagious;** soon everybody was on their feet clapping and dancing.

   Definition: _____

8. No one expected the storm to hit so suddenly, so we weren't prepared for the confusion; for a few hours everything was in complete **chaos.**

   Definition: _____

9. The news of the accident sent a wave of **shock** throughout the community; the **trauma** that people felt lasted for a long time.

   Definitions: _____
   _____

10. John's leg was broken in the accident, so they needed to carry him on a **stretcher** to the **ambulance** standing by to take him to the hospital.

    Definitions: _____
    _____

Follow-Up

The activities in this section will give you a chance to find out more about the topic of this unit and conduct some investigations of your own. You can work on some or all or just one of these activities. There are activities that you can work on alone or with others. You can adapt these activities to meet your needs; you may even think of projects of your own to undertake.

When you study language you often learn about things in life you never knew before.

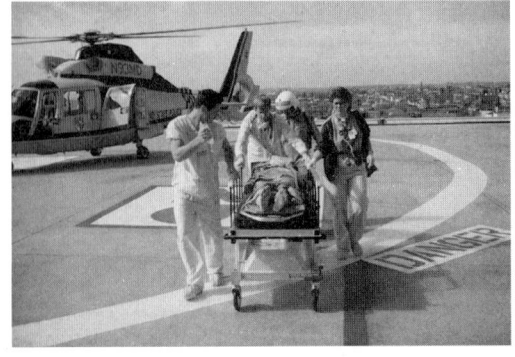

Photo courtesy of Maryland's Emergency Medical System

Follow-Up A 13

ACTIVITY TEN   Gathering Information from Reading

Step 1. Read the following questions and think about possible answers. Discuss your ideas with a partner.

1. What problems do hospital emergency rooms have to contend with today?

2. How many people used emergency rooms in the past year?

3. What are the working conditions like in emergency rooms?

4. What experiences changed emergency room medicine? What lessons were learned from these experiences?

5. What was the necessity that led to the creation of trauma units?

6. How effective have these units proved to be?

7. What hope motivated hospitals to create trauma units? What, in fact, has been the experience of hospital trauma units?

8. How did government manage to make the situation worse?

9. Why have hospitals closed intensive care units (ICUs)? What effect have these closures had on other units and on patients?

10. Which part of the population is most likely to have to use an emergency ward?

11. Why do some people still choose the emergency room rather than a clinic?
   _____
   _____

12. What has been happening in emergency rooms in urban areas?
   _____
   _____

13. According to this article, what are the solutions to the crisis of emergency room care in the United States?
   _____
   _____

Step 2. Read the text and locate the sections of the reading which contain information related to each question. Highlight or underline these sections and mark the question number in the margin.

Do You Want to Die?
by Nancy Gibbs

In large cities and small towns, the emergency room is the abused child of American medicine. Overburdened, understaffed and underfinanced, emergency departments across the country are reeling from multiple blows. Start with 37 million patients who have no health insurance. Add a graying population with a growing need for expensive treatment. Subtract government reimbursements, which often cover only half the cost of treating the poor. Factor in the effects of the AIDS epidemic and drug violence. Under such pressures, the miracle is that the system shows any vital signs at all.

Fighting hard to keep it alive are some 110,000 doctors and nurses, plus technicians, social workers and paramedics, employed by roughly 5,700 emergency departments nationwide. Last year they treated 90 million patients for everything from hangnails to heart attacks. In the busiest hospitals, emergency-room personnel minister to an average of 200 patients in a single, brutal twelve-hour shift, while stretchers stack up in the waiting rooms, hallways and even closets. Staffers eat large meals before going on duty, since there will be no breaks once they start. They treat wounds they hoped never to see outside a war zone: it is to Los Angeles, which had more automatic-weapons victims than Beirut last year, that the U.S. Army sends its physicians for combat training, at Martin Luther King Jr./Drew Medical Center. "What gives out is not patient care," says Dr. Elisabeth Rosenthal of New York Hospital, "but our sanity."

... A generation ago, emergency rooms were dumping grounds for bad doctors and training grounds for young ones. But the experience of two world wars, Korea and especially Vietnam taught doctors that saving injured patients depended as much on speed as on skill. Doctors refer to "the golden hour" after a trauma, before irreversible shock sets in, when lifesaving treatment is most likely to succeed. Beginning in the early '80s, states organized themselves into trauma networks and began tailoring training programs for physicians interested in emergency care as a specialty. The goal was not entirely altruistic: the hope was that most accident victims would be middle class and well insured.

"A lot of hospitals looked to trauma victims as $250,000 pieces of meat, and everyone wanted them," says Fred Hurtado, president of the United Paramedics of Los Angeles.

Whatever the hospitals' motives, the advantages for patients were obvious. Trauma is the leading cause of death for people under 44, killing more than 140,000 in the U.S. each year. By improving paramedic training, integrating ambulance services and diverting critical patients to hospitals that specialize in burns or limb reattachment or spinal injury, death rates could be dramatically reduced. In the year after setting up their trauma networks, Peoria, Ill., saw traffic fatalities drop 50%, and Orange County, Calif., saw deaths among non-head-injured auto-accident victims drop from an estimated 73% to 9%.

But in gearing up their emergency-care capacity, hospitals didn't bargain on a crucial economic fact: in the cities, at least, the patients most likely to need such treatment are least likely to be able to pay. Hospitals have always subsidized nonpaying patients by tacking excess charges on to bills of those with health insurance. But when it comes to emergency care, hospitals cannot handpick their clientele. A 1986 law forbids hospitals to turn away poor patients at the emergency room before they are "stabilized." The typical trauma-patient bill last year was $13,000; on average, hospitals took a loss of $5,000 on each. Says Dr. Robert Hockberger of Harbor-UCLA: "It's amazing to me that in 1983 all the hospitals didn't realize that most of the people who shoot and stab each other and wreck their cars at 3 a.m. don't have insurance."

At the same time that the trauma centers were expanding, government subsidies were collapsing. To cap soaring health-care costs, the federal and state governments tightened the controls over how much hospitals could charge Medicare patients for any procedure. Private insurers soon followed suit, with the result that patients who have used up their quota of covered costs are often discharged too early—only to return sooner and sometimes sicker to the emergency room.

Under pressure to contain their costs, many hospitals began eliminating beds, including some in their intensive-care units. ICU beds are the most expensive because they must be vigorously monitored by nurses. But by cutting back on ICU beds, hospitals simply shifted the burden to emergency rooms and other facilities. "A young man who needed neurosurgery waited eight days before he could get a bed," says Dr. Albert Lauro, director of emergency medicine at New Orleans Charity Hospital. "Another woman, who had had a stroke, waited four days. They sit in the emergency department hours and days trying to get into the intensive-care units."

In some cases, private hospitals dump expensive patients on public facilities—not because the private institutions are losing money but because they are not making as much money as they are accustomed to. "Hospitals have shifted resources away from emergency care to drug and alcohol rehabilitation or outpatient psychiatric care," says Dr. Hockberger. "These are the things that make money." According to the National Association for Hospital Development, by the year 2000, 40% of the nation's 2,200 acute-care hospitals will be closed or converted to other uses.

At the heart of the problem, health-care experts agree, is the absence of any national consensus or policy on how to care for the poor and underinsured. Many of those flocking to emergency rooms are working people whose employers are no longer able or willing to provide insurance. "The 9-to-5 executive with benefits can take time off to see his doctor," says Dr. Keith T.

Sivertson, director of the Johns Hopkins emergency department in Baltimore. "The poor slob mopping the floor until 4 a.m. may be sick after work, yet has to be ready to go back on the job the next day because if he doesn't work he doesn't get paid. Where does he get a doctor at 4 a.m.?" For many people the answer used to be walk-in health clinics; but when funding for these clinics started drying up, some closed their doors.

In those neighborhoods that have functioning clinics, patients may still choose the emergency room because it is open 24 hours a day or because they think the care is better. At Chicago's Michael Reese Hospital, some pregnant women wait in the parking lot until they are close to delivery so they can be admitted through the emergency room. The deluge has forced most hospitals to adapt their primary-care systems. Triage nurses divide patients into two groups: the critically ill, who must be seen immediately, and the less serious cases, which can be sent to "urgent-care centers." For millions of Americans, the emergency room has become the family doctor.

. . . The obvious solutions to emergency-room overload are expensive and controversial: give people access to affordable health care, pay nurses decently, allow doctors some flexibility in treating their patients and recognize that good preventive care is a sound investment. Though politicians may resist boosting their budgets for medical care, they might be surprised to learn that many of their constituents are willing to pay the price. According to a Gallup poll released this month, 73% of Californians who believe the government should provide better health care for the poor were willing to pay higher taxes for such expanded coverage; 84% favored mandatory employer-provided health insurance.

But in cities like New York, once again facing a crippling budget battle, the hospital crisis cannot be solved without huge new investments and new priorities. "In New York City," says Dr. Lynn of St. Luke's–Roosevelt, "we have a phrase: 'It always gets worse before it gets worse.'" By 1994, AIDS patients alone, who now fill 9% of the city's beds, will need an additional 2,300 hospital beds—the equivalent of four new hospitals. The major municipal hospitals are crumbling; private facilities are eating into their endowments in order to pay expenses. "It's a crazy way to run a health-care system," says Dr. Alexander Kuehl, director of New York Hospital's emergency room. "Either give us national health insurance or give us an entrepreneurial system, but don't play games asking private hospitals to spend endowment to take care of patients. The endowment is the future."

Another, perhaps inevitable, answer is to ration health care more scrupulously. Already many hospital administrators are arguing that less money should be spent on highly specialized care—patients with terminal conditions, babies born with multiple defects who are not expected to live long, elderly patients in need of organ transplants. "We have to let some babies die, some old people die," says Dr. John West, a trauma-care expert at the University of California at Irvine. "We have to look at the quality of life, and we have to look at the return on our health-care buck. You just can't keep everyone alive forever."

But the decisions and solutions will not come easily or soon. AIDS will not be cured tomorrow, nor will the population cease to age. Drugs will continue to kill, as will people who use them. When the doctors and nurses who devote themselves to saving lives on the edge are also asked to be baby-sitters, bodyguards, street fighters and traffic cops, the burnout rate will only increase. And the last thing that a grievously wounded or ailing person needs to think about in a speeding ambulance is whether the hospital doors will be open when it arrives. Until the emergency room is made safe for emergencies, no one will be safe.

"Do You Want to Die?" by Nancy Gibbs, 5/28/90, Copyright 1990 Time Inc. Reprinted by permisssion

Step 3. Discuss your answers with a partner or in groups. Refer to the text to confirm your answers. After you have located and agreed on the information which related to the question, write your answer.

Step 4. What do you think about the problems of and solutions for providing emergency care? Write your ideas on the lines below.

_____
_____
_____
_____

If possible, discuss your ideas with others.

ACTIVITY ELEVEN — Conducting Interviews

Now that you have heard and read about emergency medical services, think of some questions to ask about the availability and quality of emergency medical services in your area. Your task in this activity will be to construct a small survey and speak to the people responsible for these services who can answer your questions. You may want to work with a partner or in small groups.

Begin by identifying who you are going to speak to in your survey. You should not call the emergency service numbers or the 911 system itself. These lines need to be free for real emergencies. You could call the public relations departments of hospitals and fire and police departments to find out who to talk to. You could also contact the security service of your school or place of employment. You can conduct a phone interview or arrange to have a face-to-face meeting.

To carry out this activity you will do the following:

1. Brainstorm a list of seven to ten questions. To help you get started, consider this list of sample questions:

    Is there an ambulance service available? Who staffs it? What is its average response time?

    What is the average waiting time in an emergency room (ER) if you have to be admitted to the hospital?

    How many hospital emergency rooms are open 24 hours a day? Are they staffed by doctors 24 hours a day?

    Are the ER doctors and nurses trained in emergency medicine?

2. Discuss your questions with a partner. Change any questions that are not clear or add new questions to your list.

3. Speak to the people who can give you the information you need. Write the information you get in note form. If possible, record your face-to-face interviews. Prior to conducting the interviews, to help you note the information

18 Medical Emergency 911

people give, make an interview form on which to write your questions and question numbers. Beside each question, leave blank space to note respondents' answers. A sample interview form is provided by way of example.

INTERVIEW FORM

Person Interviewed	Question #	Answer (Note Form)
1. Les Green, Public Rel. Dir. County Hospital	#1. What hrs. is Emer. open?	24 hrs.
	#2.	

4. Read over or listen to the tapes of your interviews and prepare a short oral or written report about what you learned. To do this, first organize the information you gathered. Group together all the facts relating to the same point. List the related details in note form.
5. Make an oral presentation and/or submit your report in writing.

ACTIVITY TWELVE Using Your Skills at Home

The skills you used to gather information will improve with more listening. There are other programs in this edition of RadioWaves to listen to. In addition, you can listen to the television or radio programs that come into your home every day. Your task in this activity is to listen to and report on a television or radio program you tuned into.

There are many news or information programs that report on health stories. Look at your local television listings over the next few days and try to find a health program related to the topic of this program—emergency medical services—or a show about another health topic. You might find a news show or an entertainment show.

Step 1. Watch the program and, as you listen, write notes about the important ideas you hear. If you are able to, write any details about these ideas. If you cannot write enough as you listen and want to add more, do so after the program has concluded or during the commercial breaks. Use this note-taking form to get information about the program:

Name of Program:

Broadcast station:

Date/Time of Viewing:

Factual Information Given:

(Write notes about five or six of the most important ideas you heard.)

Questions This Show Raised:

Questions This Show Answered:

Questions This Show Left Unanswered:

Step 2. Prepare three discussion questions based on the ideas you heard.

Step 3. Present the program to a discussion group and, after the presentation, lead a discussion on the topic.

If you are working with others who watched the same show, you can compare your notes and discuss what you heard. Opportunities for listening are all around you.

SUGGESTIONS FOR OTHER FOLLOW-UP ACTIVITIES

Speaking: Group Activities

- Debate or panel discussion:
  "Hospitals Must Keep Their Emergency Rooms Open"
- Problem-solving task:
  Given a fixed hospital budget, determine priorities for funding different departments.

Individual Activities

- Three-minute talk:
  Prepare a speech that focuses on the challenges of providing emergency care. You may tape or orally present your talk.

Writing: Individual Activities

- Summary of "Medical Emergency 911"
- Expository essay:
  "The Reasons We Must Provide Emergency Care"

Listening: Individual/Group Activities

- Invite someone in the health care field to speak to your class or attend a lecture on health care issues.

Butting Out in the Board Room

2

OVERVIEW

Preparing to Listen

Activity One	Discussion Questions
Activity Two	Examining the Statistics
Activity Three	Predictions; Bridge to Listening

Listening to the Tape

Activity Four	Listening for the Main Ideas
Activity Five	Note Taking
Activity Six	Comprehension Questions

Language Close Up

Activity Seven	Language Focus: Informal Talk
Activity Eight	Language Focus: Verbs and Verb Forms
Activity Nine	Vocabulary: Guessing Meaning from Context

Follow-Up

Activity Ten	Gathering Information from Reading
Activity Eleven	Preparing a Survey

22 Butting Out in the Board Room

If you've ever tried to quit smoking or convince a friend or coworker to do so, you know what a struggle giving up cigarettes can be. This unit looks at one of the only programs in the United States that successfully supports workers who, because of company no-smoking policies, have to stop smoking. You will hear from company executives who have brought the program into their workplace, from workers who have tried the program, and from the woman who conducts the seminars as they explain how the program works. The activities will help you to understand and use the information you listen to.

Preparing to Listen

Getting some background information and thinking about the topic before you hear the program will help you to understand the ideas more easily. Complete the activities in this section **before you listen.**

ACTIVITY ONE   Discussion Questions

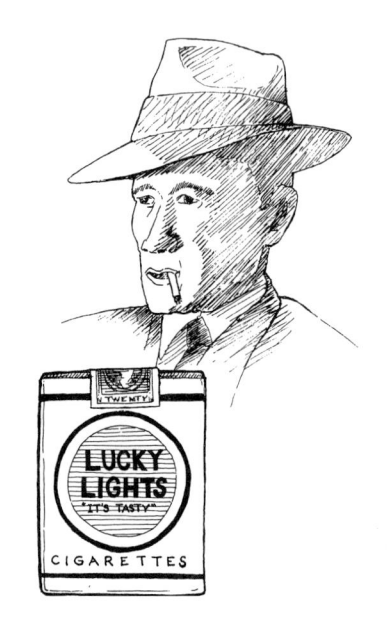

What do you think? Read and consider the following questions. Write your ideas and discuss them with others.

1. What are some ways that people are encouraged to start smoking?

2. How has smoking been promoted in the past? What kind of advertising was used on TV, radio, movies, magazines, sports events, or other promotions?

3. Why and how are people discouraged from smoking today?

4. How difficult is it for people to stop smoking?

5. What methods are used to get people to stop? How successful are these methods?

6. How are nonsmokers affected by working or living with smokers?

ACTIVITY TWO **Examining the Statistics**

Complete this activity and find out about smoking in the workplace.

Step 1. Read the following questions and decide what you think for each. Write your ideas and discuss your thoughts with a partner or partners.

1. What percentage of companies ban smoking completely or in all open work areas?

   _____

2. Why have companies introduced no-smoking policies?

   _____

3. How much do employees complain about smoking? What are companies' reactions?

   _____

4. What has happened to the morale of smokers in companies that have no-smoking policies? What have managers noticed following the adoption of no-smoking policies?

   _____

5. How do employers respond when there are employees who want to quit smoking?

   _____

6. Will the trend toward no-smoking policies for the workplace increase in the future?

   _____

Step 2. Skim (read quickly for key words) the information in these statistical reports and find the answers to the questions above.

How similar were the answers you found in the reports to the answers you predicted in Step 1?

Step 3. Discuss your answers with a partner or check the answer key.

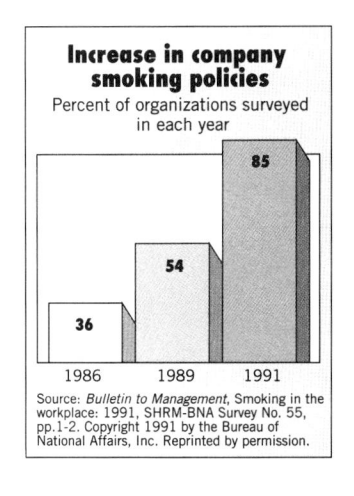

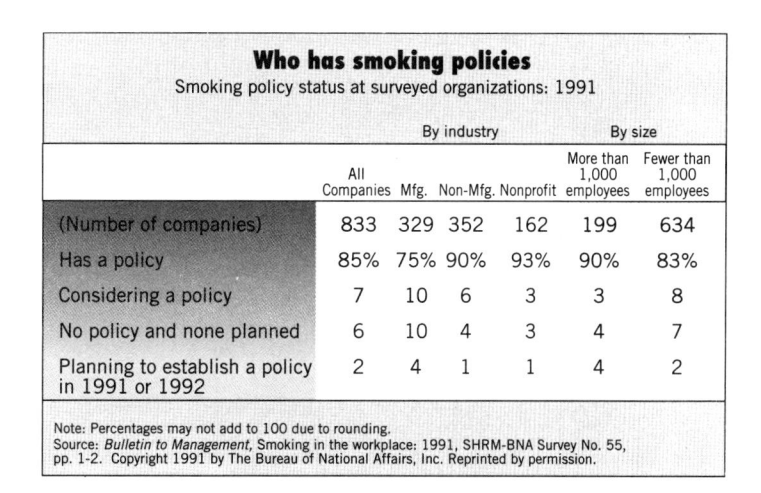

Increase in company smoking policies
Percent of organizations surveyed in each year

1986	1989	1991
36	54	85

Source: *Bulletin to Management*, Smoking in the workplace: 1991, SHRM-BNA Survey No. 55, pp.1-2. Copyright 1991 by the Bureau of National Affairs, Inc. Reprinted by permission.

Who has smoking policies
Smoking policy status at surveyed organizations: 1991

	All Companies	By industry			By size	
		Mfg.	Non-Mfg.	Nonprofit	More than 1,000 employees	Fewer than 1,000 employees
(Number of companies)	833	329	352	162	199	634
Has a policy	85%	75%	90%	93%	90%	83%
Considering a policy	7	10	6	3	3	8
No policy and none planned	6	10	4	3	4	7
Planning to establish a policy in 1991 or 1992	2	4	1	1	4	2

Note: Percentages may not add to 100 due to rounding.
Source: *Bulletin to Management*, Smoking in the workplace: 1991, SHRM-BNA Survey No. 55, pp. 1-2. Copyright 1991 by The Bureau of National Affairs, Inc. Reprinted by permission.

Butting Out in the Board Room

> **More companies are starting to curb work place smoking**
>
> The number of employers adopting work place smoking policies has more than doubled since 1986. Today, 85% of employers have smoking policies, up from 54% in 1987 and 36% in 1986, according to a 1991 survey by The Bureau of National Affairs, a business research organization, and the Society for Human Resource Management, both in Washington.
>
> Other survey findings:
> - Smoking is banned at 34% of companies, up from 7% in 1987 and 2% in 1986. Another 34% prohibit smoking in all open work areas.
> - Most organizations ban smoking in hallways (90%); restrooms (87%); conference rooms (85%); private offices (63%); employee lounges (62%); and cafeterias (59%).
> - Concerns about health prompted 79% of all policies; state or local laws were factors in 36%.
> - About 49% of all companies have received complaints from their employees about smoking. Typically, management resolves the problems by improving policy communication with employees, adding restrictions, and enforcing existing policies more strictly.
> - Morale among nonsmokers has improved (69%); among smokers, 27% have experienced a decline in morale. Managers have noticed that smokers' breaks have become longer or more frequent in half of the firms with smoking policies.
> - About 64% of companies offer help and encouragement to employees who want to quit smoking. The assistance has included distributing literature, sponsoring stop-smoking programs, or offering incentives.
> - Among employers without smoking policies, 16% plan to adopt one in 1992; 44% have policies under consideration.
>
> Source: Bulletin to Management, Smoking in the Workplace: 1991, SHRM-BNA Survey No.55. Copyright 1991 by The Bureau of National Affairs, Inc. Used with permission.

ACTIVITY THREE Predictions; Bridge to Listening

Part One: Predictions

Based on the ideas you have thought about and discussed so far, make a few predictions about the ideas you expect to find out about in this program.

Write your ideas on the lines below. You can write your ideas in either words or phrases; in question or answer form. Write any ideas your have. Don't worry about whether they are good or bad or whether they are correctly written. A prediction is given as an example to help you get started.

1. What is unique about this program? What methods does it use?
2. _____
3. _____
4. _____
5. _____

Discuss your predictions. Later, you can check to see if your predictions were accurate.

Part Two: Bridge to Listening

The purpose of the introduction is to prepare you for the information in the program. It will give you an overview or a taste of something interesting to come.

Step 1. Cue your tape to the introduction of the show, which begins, "For years, the tobacco companies spread their message." Turn on the tape.

Step 2. Listen to the introduction, which ends, "a new approach to an old habit," without stopping the tape. Think about the information as you listen. Stop the tape at the end of the introduction.

Step 3. From what you recall, answer as many questions as possible in note form. The first is given as an example.

1. What message have tobacco companies spread over the years? When and why did this situation change?

    Smoking-popular/change 1964/cancer

2. How many people in the United States still smoke? Why is this a problem for them?

3. What are some companies in Milwaukee, Wisconsin, doing to help their employees?

Discuss your ideas with a partner. Check the answer key. Compare these ideas to the predictions you made before.

Listening to the Tape

The activities in this section will help you to practice your skills in understanding and using the information you hear. Concentrate on the task you have to accomplish and practice the skills, such as note taking or listening for details, needed to complete the task. Remember the strategies for coping with listening to radio reports listed on page 5:

- Focus on what you understand.
- Don't worry about information that goes by quickly.
- Share information and clarify what you're not sure of.

Note Taking

In many of the activities that follow you will be identifying the main points and details and often writing what you hear in note form. These activities will help you get more of the important information in your notes more quickly.

For a few tips about writing quick notes as you listen, read the information on page 6. For more complete information about improving your note-taking skills, refer to the Guide to Note Taking (Appendix 1, p. 93).

ACTIVITY FOUR   Listening for the Main Ideas

Step 1. Listen to the program "Butting Out in the Board Room" without stopping. Think about the information as you listen. Stop the tape at the end of the program. Write three main ideas that you heard in note form.

1. _____
2. _____
3. _____

Step 2. Discuss your ideas with a partner or check the answer key.

ACTIVITY FIVE — Note Taking

This report is about the "Coping Without Smoking" program developed by the American Lung Association of Wisconsin. This report is relatively well organized in that it focuses on three main ideas. Each idea is explained before the report turns to the next point. Some radio reports, like most good academic talks, follow an organization such as this.

As you listen to and follow the report, use a divided-page note-taking format listing main ideas, supporting points, and details. To help you organize the information, sample notes are provided that list the report's first main idea, second main idea, third main idea, and its conclusion. The sample notes provide supporting points and details to describe the first main idea, and supporting points (but no details) for the second main idea. For the third main idea and the conclusion, only the main ideas are given. Your job is to provide the rest. If necessary, take notes on a separate sheet of paper.

Step 1. Read the note-taking form before you begin. Think about the details you could note. If possible, discuss them with a partner.

Step 2. Rewind the tape to the beginning of the program "Butting Out in the Board Room." Listen without stopping. Take notes on as much of the information as you can.

You may not be able to write as much as you would like. Don't worry—you'll be able to write more notes as you get more opportunities to listen, and the percentage of information you can jot down in notes will increase with each program.

Main Ideas	Supporting Points, Details

A. No-smoking policy at Warner Cable Company	—Policy adopted
	—Reason for policy
	    —second-hand smoke, lung cancer
	    —harmful for non-smokers
	—Company's statement
	    —Deidre Edwards/Human Resources Director
	—Co. decision
	    —Complete ban in building
	—Workers affected
	    —50%
	    —Some willing/some not
	—Ex.: Jenny Mueller

B. Coping without smoking/ Program	—Cathy Hoffman/program developer — — —

Main Ideas	Supporting Points	Details

—Seminars conducted

—
—
 —Techniques:
—Characteristics of seminars
—
—
—
—
—What Hoffman says of program
—
—
—
—Reaction from employees:
—
C. Marsh Electronics/   —Employee no. 2
    No-smoking policy

D. Conclusion

Step 3. Stop the tape at the end of the program and read over your notes. If you have a partner, discuss what you heard and wrote. As you read or discuss, add more information to your notes.

Step 4 (Optional). Listen another time to confirm and complete your notes. Read your notes and discuss again.

ACTIVITY SIX   Comprehension Questions

Answering these questions correctly is a check on the accuracy of your listening.

Step 1. Read the following questions. Use your notes to answer as many questions as possible. Write the answers to these questions **in note form.** The first question is completed by way of example.

1. Why are more companies in the United States adopting no-smoking policies?

   health studies/2nd-hand smoke- to cancer

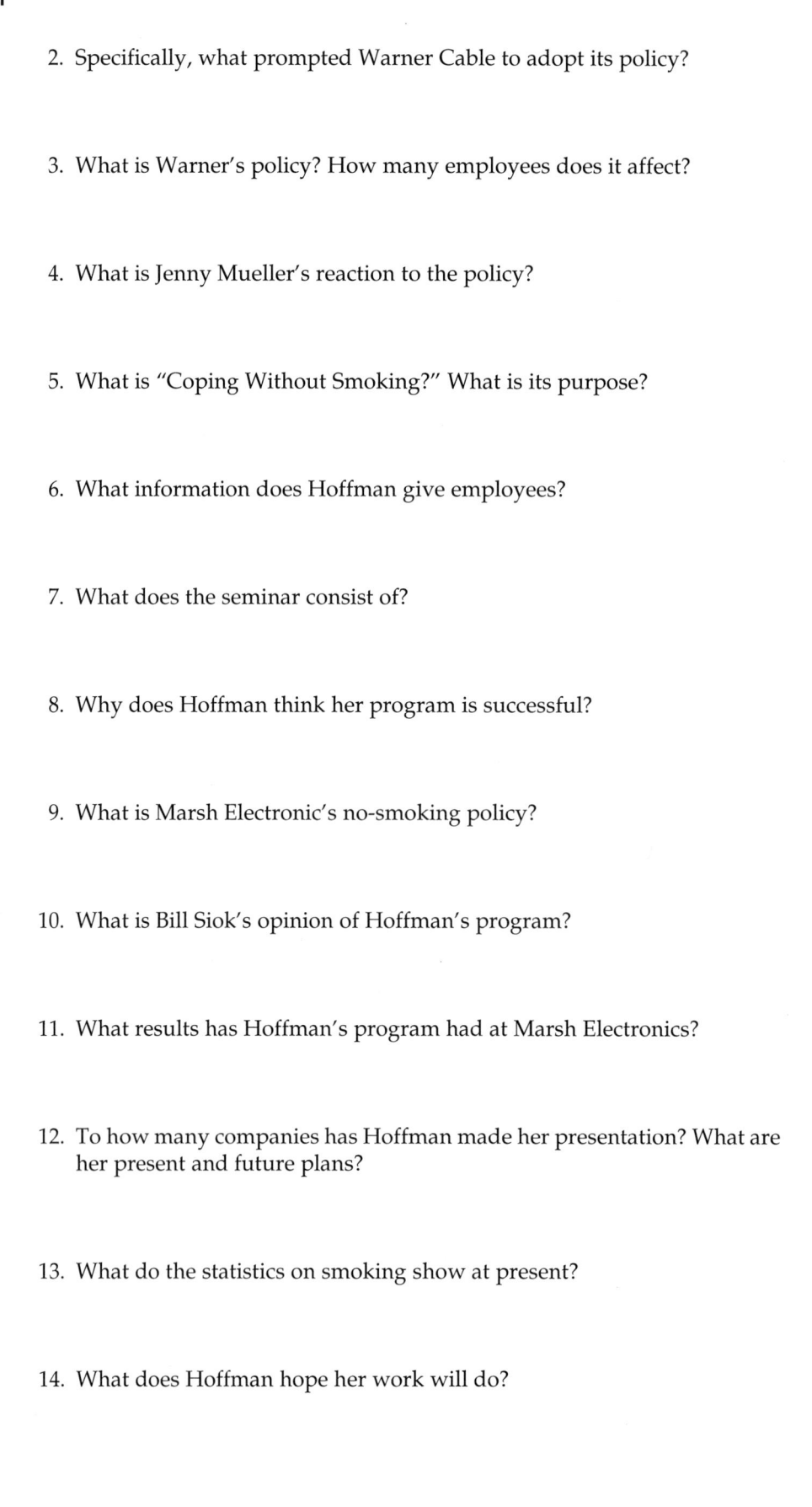

2. Specifically, what prompted Warner Cable to adopt its policy?

3. What is Warner's policy? How many employees does it affect?

4. What is Jenny Mueller's reaction to the policy?

5. What is "Coping Without Smoking?" What is its purpose?

6. What information does Hoffman give employees?

7. What does the seminar consist of?

8. Why does Hoffman think her program is successful?

9. What is Marsh Electronic's no-smoking policy?

10. What is Bill Siok's opinion of Hoffman's program?

11. What results has Hoffman's program had at Marsh Electronics?

12. To how many companies has Hoffman made her presentation? What are her present and future plans?

13. What do the statistics on smoking show at present?

14. What does Hoffman hope her work will do?

Step 2. Discuss the information with others.

Step 3 (Optional). If you need to, listen to the program to find answers that you don't have or can't agree upon. Stop the tape when you hear the information you are listening for and write your answer.

Language Close Up

In this section you can practice listening for specific language. The activities focus on different features, such as improving your awareness of grammatical form or improving your ability to hear key details. The activities will help you to be more aware of the different tones, colloquial expressions, and speaking styles people use when they talk. You can learn vocabulary through the practice of guessing meaning from context.

ACTIVITY SEVEN Language Focus: Informal Talk

In this program people were speaking informally to give information, react to questions, or talk about their feelings. When people are speaking informally it is harder to follow. Sometimes people slide words together or use words like "um" or "ah" while they think of what to say next, or they may repeat the same word twice before finishing their thought. In this activity you will follow these steps:

Step 1. Listen to parts of the tape in which people are speaking informally.

Step 2. Fill in the blanks.

Step 3. Language features: Decide if the speakers are

   a. Giving information.

   b. Reacting to a question.

   c. Talking about their feelings.

Step 4. Write the informal language in standard English.
Cue your tape to the beginning of each numbered section.

1. "It's _____ be hard at work though, when it's a stressful situation. That's _____ _____ . There's certain, um, _____ _____ happen, and _____ , _____ light up, and that's _____ _____ be really hard, I think."

    A. Choose one: The speakers are
       a. Giving information.
       b. Reacting to a question.
       c. Talking about their feelings.

    B. Choose two examples of informal speech (eg., words that slide together) and write them in standard English.

    _____

    _____

30 Butting Out in the Board Room

2. "Some of the techniques _____ , like the rubber

   band around the wrist or, um, the cinnamon stick to

   _____ , _____ like that. And also, um,

   _____ stop and think why _____ smok-

   ing. I think _____ a big thing too."

   A. Choose one: The speakers are
      a. Giving information.
      b. Reacting to a question.
      c. Talking about their feelings.
   B. Choose two examples of informal speech and write them in standard English.

   _____

   _____

3. The exercise _____ on

   _____ , and ah,

   _____ just _____ my

   mind towards _____

   _____ . Every time I think, about

   _____ cigarette I think of something

   positive that I can get out of it."

   A. Choose one: The speakers are
      a. Giving information.
      b. Reacting to a question.
      c. Talking about their feelings.
   B. Choose two examples of informal speech and write them in standard English.

   _____

   _____

ACTIVITY EIGHT   Language Focus: Verbs and Verb Forms

Read the next sections of the transcript, in which the reporter talks about Cathy Hoffman's seminars. What verbs or verb forms are used?

Before listening, read and complete any of the missing information you can remember from the following part of the transcript.

Cue to the beginning of each numbered section.

1. Hoffman _____ seminars like this one in

   business after business in Wisconsin, _____

   employees the steps they _____ _____ to _____

to the new nonsmoking policy. She _____ them to _____ walks, _____ on carrot sticks, even _____ rubber bands around their wrists; anything to _____ their mind off cigarettes.

2. Hoffman usually _____ to small groups, but sometimes as many as forty people _____ _____ _____. Her seminars _____ about an hour and a half. They _____ two short videos and some written materials _____ the health risks of smoking and tips for _____ the habit. She _____ her program is low key and that _____ why it _____.

Read over and complete the segment you heard. If you need to, listen again. If you are working in a pair, read the segment to your partner. If you are working alone, check your work against the transcript. You can read the segment along with your tape and try to imitate the speaker.

ACTIVITY NINE Vocabulary: Guessing Meaning from Context

You have heard each of the words **in bold print** as you listened to the program. In this activity you will focus on the language used and guess the meaning of these words from the context in which they are used.

DIRECTIONS

Step 1. Read each sentence. Based on your understanding of the sentence, try to guess what the word or words mean.

Step 2. Write your own definition for the words in bold print. You can check your definition with a partner or consult your dictionary.

1. They discussed the new rules and everyone wanted them to be accepted, so they were **adopted** without exception.

    Definition: _____

2. She never smoked, but since her husband often smoked at home, she was in danger of falling ill from the effects of **second-hand smoke.**

    Definition: _____

3. She had never been interested in football, but her son joined the local team and this **prompted** her to find out about the sport.

    Definition: _____

4. He had never lived in a cold climate, so it took a few months for his body to **acclimate** itself to the northern part of Canada.

    Definition: _____

5. Often it was so cold that he would **tremble** to the point that even his co-workers would notice his shaking hands.

   Definition: _____

6. She was so expert a leader in her field that she was often invited to **conduct seminars** to explain her work to others.

   Definition: _____

7. His approach is very **low key;** he isn't pushy or aggressive at all.

   Definition: _____

8. The company felt that three months was a reasonable **time frame** within which its employees could complete the safety course.

   Definition: _____

9. I needed to be mentally prepared and confident for the race but I was having trouble **gearing my mind** toward winning.

   Definition: _____

10. The plan seemed to be good but it had never been tried before so we would see the benefits only after we **implemented** it.

    Definition: _____

Follow-Up

The activities in this section will give you a chance to find out more about the topic of this unit and conduct some investigations of your own. You can work on some or all or just one of these activities. There are activities that you can work on alone or with others. You can adapt these activities to meet your needs; you may even think of projects of your own to undertake.

When you study language you often learn about things in life you never knew before.

ACTIVITY TEN Gathering Information from Reading

Part One: Post-Listening/Pre-Reading Task

After listening to the program, what questions, reactions, or opinions do you have about banning smoking in the workplace and helping employees overcome their addiction to nicotine? Write your questions on the lines provided:

_____

_____

_____

_____

If possible, discuss your thoughts with others.

Part Two: Reading and Answering Questions

Step 1. Preview the text (read and highlight the main ideas). Note the main ideas in the margin. If possible, discuss these points with a partner.

The High Cost of Smoking
by Kenneth A. Moore

In his book, *Koop: Memoirs of America's Family Doctor* (Random House, 1991), former Surgeon General C. Everett Koop, M.D., recalls the surprisingly subdued reaction to his 1988 report that identified nicotine as an addictive drug.

"Perhaps the public didn't take the report to heart because the stereotyped idea of drug addiction does not include images of nicotine craving," he wrote. "While television might offer graphic images of heroin or cocaine addiction, it doesn't usually show the craving of the nicotine addict," he explained.

Koop's high-profile stance has done much to bring the dangers of smoking to the attention of the American public. Per capita cigarette consumption in the United States actually peaked at 4,345 in 1963, just prior to the Jan. 11, 1964, release of the landmark Surgeon General's report that definitively linked cigarette smoking to death and serious illness.

But in the 1980s in particular, great progress was made toward reaching Koop's widely hailed and well-publicized goal of "a smoke-free society by the year 2000."

In 1965, 50.2% of all men smoked, and by 1987, 31.7% did. Among women, 31.9% smoked in 1965; by 1987 only 26.8% did.

Nevertheless, more than 50 million Americans, or 28% of the population, still smokes. And while the good news is that the number of smokers has decreased over the past several decades, the bad news is that those who continue to smoke tend to be heavily addicted to cigarettes.

Smoking remains the leading preventable cause of death in the United States. It is responsible for more than 1,100 deaths per day—434,000 per year—more deaths than drugs, alcohol, automobile accidents, and AIDS combined.

The cost to society. The number of deaths due to smoking can be easily calculated, but the economic losses are somewhat harder to determine. Nevertheless, there have been some notable attempts to do so.

The Congressional Office of Technology Assessment in 1985 determined that smoking-related illness accounted for $22 billion in health care costs and $43 billion in lost productivity (including absenteeism and disability) for an annual total of $65 billion.

Another estimate was generated by the U.S. Department of Health and Human Services in 1990. Using a computer program developed by the Minnesota Department of Health, the report fixed the total cost to society of smoking-related illnesses at over $52 billion each year, broken down as follows:

- Direct morbidity costs (health care costs): $23.7 billion (45.2% of the total);
- Indirect morbidity costs (such as those attributed to lost income and use of home care services): $10.2 billion (19.6%);
- Indirect mortality costs (lost productivity due to premature deaths): $18.5 billion (35.2%).

The cost to employers. The price paid by individual companies to accomodate smoking in the work place is even more difficult to calculate. In 1981, William L. Weis, professor of business at Seattle University, concluded that if the costs of health care, increased fire insurance, damage to property, absenteeism and lost productivity were added together, employers were paying as much as $4,600 annually for each smoker. Today, Weis believes the figure is much higher—possibly as much as $8,000 to $10,000 per smoker.

In the mid-1980s, Control Data Corp., Minneapolis, the computer technology company, sought to determine the effect of various health risks—including smoking—on its medical plan, which is both self-insured and self-administered. In a joint study with Milliman & Robertson Inc., Brookfield, Wis., actuarial consultants, Control Data analyzed employees' medical claims from 1981 through 1984. The object of the study was to see the impact of seven different characteristics on health care costs. In addition to smoking, the study focused on exercise, weight, hypertension, alcohol use, cholesterol level, and the use of seat belts while riding in automobiles.

The results showed that people who smoked one or more packs a day experienced 18% higher medical claim costs than nonsmokers. Persons in the high-risk category [heavy smokers] not only had higher medical claims, but spent 25% more days as inpatients in hospitals, and were 29% more likely to have annual claims over $5,000 than those in the low-risk [nonsmoker] category, the study determined.

Group Health Cooperative of Puget Sound, Seattle, an HMO with 9,000 employees, made its facilities smoke-free in 1984. Timothy McAfee, M.D., coordinator of tobacco cessation services, attributes the company's decision to prohibit on-site smoking to two factors. First, because the company was known as a leader in preventive care, "it was inconsistent with our image and the emphasis we place on health care to not address the smoking issue."

But McAfee notes that the decision to ban worksite smoking was also based on costs. Adding together extra direct medical costs, absenteeism, and lost productivity, the company realized it was paying at least an additional $1,100 per year per smoker, he reports.

Lost productivity. Absenteeism related to smoking has been widely studied. In the 1980s, researchers concluded that the average smoker misses 2.2 more days of work each year than the nonsmoker.

In December 1989, a team of researchers from East Carolina University, Greenville, N.C., further tracked smoking-related absenteeism. They compared medical records of 50 smokers and 50 ex-smokers who worked at a pharmaceutical company in eastern North Carolina.

Predictably, they found that those who smoked were absent more than those who had quit. Moreover, from the point at which the former smokers had stopped smoking, their absences decreased steadily over the next three years.

Other costs of smoking. In addition to lowering costs of direct health care and decreasing losses due to absenteeism and reduced productivity, companies that enact smoking restrictions can count on still other economic benefits. Their costs of building and office maintenance, including painting, repair and replacement of furniture and carpeting with burn holes, are bound to decrease.

Moreover, while Weis of Seattle University considered smoke damage to equipment during his 1981 research, there was one factor he couldn't have taken into account at that time: the rapid computerization of American business, which took place largely in the 1980s.

"Today, every desk in an office seems to have some kind of terminal on it," he notes. Since computer equipment is highly vulnerable to contamination by smoke particles, the potential for smoke-related damage to disk drives and other expensive components is enormous. Because of the risk smoking presents to electronic equipment of all types, Weis now says, "the thought of accommodating smoking seems ridiculous."

Trying to accommodate smokers by setting up designated smoking areas is also costly, Weis says. He points out that the federal Environmental Protection Agency recommends that buildings in which people smoke have separate ventilation systems, so that smoke can be sucked out of the building. "Air displacement rates for smoking areas must be five to seven times higher than for smoke-free areas. The cost of the extra energy needed to maintain those air displacement rates is high," he says.

Passive smoking. As compelling as all of these cost-related data are, it's interesting to note that only since the Surgeon General reported on the link between passive smoking and illness have most states and businesses begun to restrict smoking.

Environmental tobacco smoke, or ETS, as passive smoke is often called, is a combination of exhaled smoke, and "sidestream" smoke emitted from a burning tobacco product between puffs. In 1988, the Surgeon General concluded that involuntary smoking is a cause of disease, including lung cancer, in nonsmokers.

Koop clearly advocated policies that guaranteed nonsmokers the right to breathe air free of tobacco smoke. "The right of smokers to smoke ends when their behavior affects the health and well-being of others," he wrote.

Various studies throughout the 1980s placed the number of lung cancer deaths attributable to ETS in the range of about 3,000 to 5,000 annually. In 1992, Kyle Steenland, senior epidemiologist for methods development of the National Institute for Occupation Safety and Health, Cincinnati, reported that as many as 35,000 to 40,000 annual heart disease deaths can also be attributed to ETS.

In 1988, Koop advocated efforts to help smokers quit smoking. He wrote, "It doesn't make sense to me for an insurance company to fork over $150,000 for a client's terminal illness with lung cancer, but not be willing to put up $64 or $200 to help him stop smoking and avoid lung cancer in the first place."

Apparently, many employers agree with the logic, as they seek to eliminate smoke from the work place and try to help motivated employees kick the smoking habit.

"Almost anything you do is going to help," says McAfee of Group Health Cooperative of Puget Sound. "If a class costs $100 per smoker, it may double or triple the probability that the smoker will quit. Compared with almost anything I do as a physician to treat smoking-related illness, that's an incredible bargain."

From Business & Health: Special Report, Ciba-Geigy, 1992.

Step 2. Read the following questions and discuss possible answers with a partner before rereading.

1. How much money is spent on health care for smoking-related diseases?

2. How much money is spent on lost productivity due to smoking-related absenteeism and disability?

3. What is the cost of lost productivity due to smoking-related premature death?

4. How much were employers paying annually for each smoker in 1981? How much do they pay today?

5. What were the results of Control Data's study on the effect of various health risks, including smoking?

6. What were the reasons the Group Health Cooperative in Seattle decided to make its workplace smoke-free in 1984?

7. What have studies on the cost of absenteeism due to smoking shown?

8. What happens to absenteeism when people quit smoking?

9. How has the computerization of American business influenced the decision to have a smoke-free workplace?

10. What must businesses do to set up designated smoking areas?

11. What is ETS and what are the health risks associated with it?

12. What is the economic logic behind setting up programs in the workplace to help smokers quit?

Step 3. Reread, scanning for the sections of the reading that contain information related to each question. Underline the information and mark the question number in the margin. Write your answers in note form.

Step 4. Discuss your answers with a partner or check the answer key.

ACTIVITY ELEVEN Preparing a Survey

What companies that you know of have no-smoking policies? In this activity, you will get a chance to conduct a survey and interview businesspeople to learn their opinions about workplace policies on smoking. You may carry out this activity with a partner or in small groups. To carry out this activity you will do the following:

1. Brainstorm a list of seven to ten questions to ask. You could inquire into your respondent's position on workplace smoking policies. You could ask for details about their companies' policies; for example, how strict or lenient the policies are, when and why they were introduced, their effect, and if and how they help employees quit smoking. Or you could ask their opinions on whether cigarettes should be more or less heavily taxed. There are many aspects to explore.

2. Check your questions with a partner, if you have one. Make a survey form on which the questions are written. Beside each question, leave a blank space to note respondents' answers. A sample survey form is provided by way of example.

SURVEY FORM

Person Interviewed	Question #	Answer (Note Form)
1. Charles Brown, Dir. Language Inst.	#1. What is sm. policy	smoking/ all public rms.
	#2.	

3. Choose five people to interview. Write the information you get in note form. If possible, tape record your interviews.
4. Read over your survey form and listen to the tape of your interviews to prepare a short oral report on what you found out.
5. Present your oral report to others.

SUGGESTIONS FOR OTHER FOLLOW-UP ACTIVITIES

Speaking: Group Activities

- Debate/panel discussion:
  "Companies Should Ban Smoking in the Workplace"
- Values clarification task:
  Decide if you agree or disagree with the following statements:

  Smoking is a matter of individual rights and freedoms.

  A smoking ban protects the public's right to safety.

  Tobacco companies should be held legally responsible for illness or death from diseases caused by smoking.

  Taxes on cigarettes should be increased.

Individual Activities

- Three-minute Talk:
  Prepare a speech that discusses various aspects of the smoking-policy debate. You may tape or orally present your talk.

Writing: Individual Activities

- Summary of "Butting Out in the Board Room"
- Expository essay on argument:
  "For or Against: Should Restrictions on Smoking Be Increased?"

Listening: Individual/Group Activities

- Lectures on health care issues
- At home: Listening to TV or radio broadcasts
  (See pp. 18–19 for details about this activity.)

Summer Camp for Sick Kids   3

OVERVIEW

Preparing to Listen

Activity One	Discussion Questions
Activity Two	Getting Information from Illustrations; Retells
Activity Three	Predictions; Bridge to Listening

Listening to the Tape

Activity Four	Listening for the Main Ideas
Activity Five	Writing Focused Notes
Activity Six	Comprehension Questions

Language Close Up

Activity Seven	Language Focus: Informal Speech
Activity Eight	Vocabulary: Guessing Meaning from Context

Follow-Up

Activity Nine	Gathering Information from Reading
Activity Ten	A Book Report

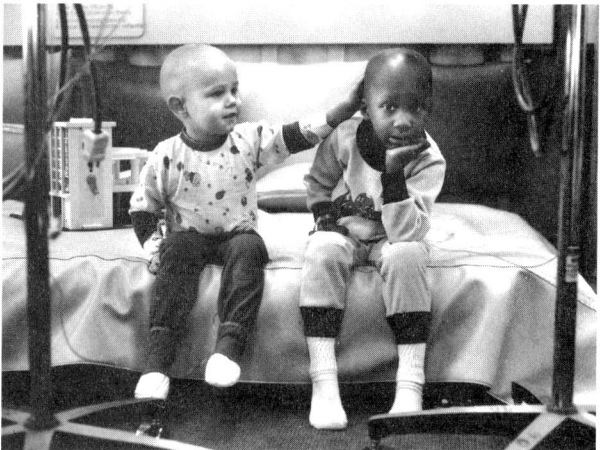

A Summer Camp for Sick Kids

Children who have serious, possibly life-threatening diseases develop ways to cope with their disease. But these kids, like all children, sometimes just want to have fun. This program brings you up close to look at a special program in the United States that successfully offers sick kids a chance to have some normal summer fun, swimming and playing, in combination with special activities that help them emotionally. You will hear kids and staff talk about their experiences. The activities will help you to understand and use the information you listen to.

Preparing to Listen

Getting some background information and thinking about the topic before you hear the program will help you to understand the ideas more easily. Complete the activities in this section **before you listen**.

ACTIVITY ONE Discussion Questions

What do you think? Read and consider the following questions. Write your ideas and discuss them with others.

1. What are some of the activities at summer camp?
   _____
   _____

2. What kinds of special services and equipment would be needed at a camp for critically ill children?
   _____
   _____

3. In what ways can a camp experience help a critically ill child?
   _____
   _____

4. In what ways can a camp for sick children help the health professionals who work there?
   _____
   _____

ACTIVITY TWO Getting Information from Illustrations; Retells

DIRECTIONS Choose one of the pictures and study it carefully. Look at the action shown in the illustration. Read the description written under the illustration. Prepare an oral description explaining what the picture shows, as well as the thoughts and emotions of the people involved and the sounds they might be hearing. Tell as much as you can.

If possible, pair up with someone who chose the same picture you did. Tell your partner what you plan to say and discuss changes or additions to your description. Then, get together with partners who prepared descriptions of the other pictures to listen to and talk about your own and the others' descriptions.

At the Hole in the Wall Gang Camp, kids get to ride and care for horses. It's a first-time experience for many and a dream come true for children who may have been spending more of their time in a hospital clinic than a Western-style corral. *Note:* The Camp is named after the hideout of the outlaw Butch Cassidy, who was portrayed by Paul Newman in the movie *Butch Cassidy and the Sundance Kid.*

Pia loves to swim but she has sickle-cell anemia and can't tolerate cool water. At the camp the pool is heated to 85°F and there are blankets and sunlamps to warm her when she gets out of the water.

The company of their counselor and the quiet of the lake offer a chance for two young campers to relax and try their hand at fishing. The lake is well stocked, so getting a catch is no problem; often the young fishermen throw their catch back in the water. The camp is designed to give sick kids the kinds of camp experiences that children of all ages love and learn from. It is the first camp in the United States especially designed to meet the needs of sick children.

The camp is the inspiration of actor Paul Newman. The buildings are designed in a combination of American folk styles that reflect different regional influences. They create a warm and homey environment that is tailored to meet the needs of kids with serious diseases without looking or feeling like a medical facility. Even the camp infirmary looks like a movie set.

Photos courtesy of the Hole in the Wall Gang.

42 ▲ Summer Camp for Sick Kids

ACTIVITY THREE ## Predictions; Bridge to Listening

Part One: Predictions

Based on what you know about the subject so far, what information would you predict this program will give you about the Hole in the Wall Gang Camp?

Write your ideas on the lines below. You can write your ideas in either words or phrases, in question or sentence form. Write any ideas you have. Don't worry about whether they are good or bad or whether they are correctly written.

1. _____
2. _____
3. _____
4. _____

Discuss your predictions. Later, you can check to see if your predictions were accurate.

Part Two: Bridge to Listening

The purpose of the introduction is to prepare you for the information in the program. It will give you an overview or a taste of something interesting to come.

Step 1. Cue your tape to the introduction of the show, which begins, "Every summer thousands of children." Turn on the tape.

Step 2. Listen to the introduction, which ends, "one camper for whom the camp has made all the difference" without stopping the tape. Think about the information as you listen. Stop the tape at the end of the introduction.

Step 3. From what you recall, answer as many questions as possible in note form. The first answer is given as an example.

1. Where do many children go every summer?

    New England/overnight camp

2. What activities at the Hole in the Wall Gang Camp are similar to other camps?

3. What activities are featured at the Hole in the Wall Gang Camp that are special to this camp?

Discuss your ideas with a partner or check the answer key. Compare these ideas with the predictions you made before.

▲▲▲▲▲▲▲▲▲▲▲▲▲▲▲▲▲▲▲▲

Listening to the Tape

The activities in this section will help you to practice your skills in understanding and using the information you hear. Concentrate on the task you have to accomplish and practice the skills (for example, note taking) needed to complete the task. Remember the strategies for coping with listening to radio reports listed on page 5:

- Focus on what you understand.
- Don't worry about information that goes by quickly.
- Share information and clarify what you're not sure of.

Note Taking

In many of the activities that follow you will be identifying the main ideas, supporting points, and details and often writing what you hear in note form. These activities will help you get more of the important information in your notes more quickly.

For a few tips about writing quick notes as you listen, read the information on page 6. For more complete information about improving your note-taking skills, refer to the Guide to Note Taking (Appendix 1, p. 93).

ACTIVITY FOUR Listening for the Main Ideas

Step 1. Listen to the program "Summer Camp for Sick Kids" without stopping. Number the following main ideas according to the order in which you hear them.

( ) **A.** Description of the camp

( ) **B.** Pia's experience at camp

( ) **C.** Medical problems of children at the camp

( ) **D.** Purpose of the camp

Step 2. Discuss your answers with a partner or check the answer key.

ACTIVITY FIVE Writing Focused Notes

When you listen to a radio report you hear a wonderful mix of voices and sounds. The information you hear is a mixture of factual information blended with opinion and emotion. A radio report isn't always organized in the same logical pattern as a good academic lecture. It follows a pattern of describing or explaining the important ideas (main points and details) related to the topic, from the reporter's point of view.

Your task is to listen and take notes so you will be able to explain the main points and important details of this report to someone who has questions about the Hole in the Wall Gang Camp. Your notes will help you to discuss the details of what you heard.

DIRECTIONS To take focused notes follow these steps:

Step 1. Read the following general questions and think about the information you heard. What details can you recall?

1. What kinds of activities does this summer camp offer campers like Pia?
2. How can you describe Pia and the disease she has? How does it affect her?

44 A Summer Camp for Sick Kids

3. What are the camp's location and characteristics? What kids does it serve?
4. Who is the medical director? What do doctors and nurses learn at the camp?
5. What opportunities and experiences can people have at the camp?

Step 2. If possible, discuss these questions with others. Write the ideas you recall in notes (supporting points or details).

Step 3. Rewind to the beginning of the program. Start the tape. As you listen, write supporting points and details in note form for each of the questions you have just discussed.

Read the sample notes to see what kind of detail is important and how to write in note form. Try taking notes for the first question yourself as you listen to the tape. Compare what you have written to the sample notes provided. Your wording may not be the same, but the ideas should be.

1. What kinds of activities does this summer camp offer campers?

Description of Camp Activities

-writing a story/dandelion
-1/2 doz. campers/counselors/
　at gazebo/by pond
-Creative Writing Workshop
　　-Pia/19 yrs. old
　　　-not typical
　　　-came '88/first not happy/thought-stay nurse-watch

You may not be able to write as much as you would like. Don't worry—you'll be able to write more notes as you get more opportunities to listen, and the percentage of information you can jot down in notes will increase with practice.

2. How can you describe Pia and the disease she has? How does it affect her?

3. What are the camp's location and characteristics? What kids does it serve?

4. Who is the medical director? What do doctors and nurses learn at the camp?

5. What opportunities and experiences can people have at the camp?

Step 4. Stop the tape at the end of the program and read your notes. If you have a partner, discuss what you heard and wrote. As you read or discuss, add information to your notes.

Step 5 (Optional). Listen another time to confirm and complete your notes. Read and discuss again.

ACTIVITY SIX   Comprehension Questions

Answering these questions correctly is a check on the accuracy of your listening.

Step 1. Read the following questions and use your notes to answer as many of them as possible. Write the answers to these questions **in note form.** See question 1 for an example of how to do this.

1. Where is the Hole in the Wall Gang Camp located?

    -Ashford, CT
    -1/2 hr. from Hartford

2. What did Pia Taylor think the camp would be like when she first came?

3. How is Pia described?

4. What is sickle-cell anemia?

5. What problem has Pia had with most swimming pools? How is the pool at Hole in the Wall different?

6. What was Pia's reaction to her experience in the pool?

7. What is the camp like? What special equipment does it have?

8. When did the camp open? How many kids have attended?

9. What is Dr. Pearson's role? What is his specialty?

10. What did Dr. Pearson find out about kids with sickle-cell anemia?

11. Who does the camp have on staff?

12. What has the camp meant to Pia?

13. What are Paul Newman's hopes and plans for the future of camps like Hole in the Wall?

Step 2. Discuss the information with others.

Step 3 (Optional). If you need to, listen to the program to find answers that were not in your notes. Stop the tape when you hear the information you are listening for and write your answer.

Language Close Up

In this section you can practice listening for specific language. The activities focus on different features, such as improving your awareness of grammatical form and improving your ability to hear key details. The activities will help you to be more aware of the different tones, colloquial expressions, and speaking styles people use when they talk. You can learn vocabulary through the practice of guessing meaning from context.

ACTIVITY SEVEN

Language Focus: Informal Speech

In this program Pia speaks to the reporter about her feelings and experiences at the camp. When people are speaking informally it is harder to follow their speech; sometimes people slide words together and say "I wanna" instead of "I want to," or use words like "hey" or "like" while they think of what to say next; or they may repeat a word or phrase before finishing their thought. In this activity you will listen to parts of the tape in which Pia is speaking informally.

Your task is to listen and circle the words or phrases that are spoken in an informal way.

Cue your tape to the beginning of the following section.

"I came here in '88. I wasn't all ecstatic about it. I just knew it was like some . . . they're just, they're just acting crazy, that's all. And I know it's going to be like Girl Scout or 4-H camp, and I'm going to be stuck to the nurse's side or whatever, you know . . . just sitting at the sidelines watching everybody play."

Pause the tape and discuss the words or phrases you circled. Discuss the features of each.

Are they

Words that slide together,

False starts (repeated or incomplete ideas),

Fragments (part of the sentence is left out), or

Interruptors (ah, um, you know) that characterize informal speech?

Follow-Up (Optional)

Are there other parts of the tape in which the speaker is using informal speech? Choose a section that you may have found difficult to understand and circle the words or phrases that show some of the features of spoken language. Discuss these with a partner, if possible.

ACTIVITY EIGHT   Vocabulary: Guessing Meaning from Context

You have heard the words **in bold print** in the program. In this activity you will focus on the language used and guess the meaning of these words from the context in which they are used.

DIRECTIONS

Step 1. Read each sentence. Based on your understanding of the sentence, try to guess what the word or words mean.

Step 2. Write your own definition for the words in bold print. You can check your definition with a partner or consult your dictionary.

1. They built the **gazebo** in the garden, where they could sit and enjoy the flowers.

   Definition: _____

2. The weight of the bridge was supported by the steel **trestles** she built.

   Definition: _____

3. She was **ecstatic**—so happy that she couldn't stop smiling.

   Definition: _____

4. He had injured his arm and couldn't play on the team, so he sat on the **sidelines** and watched the game.

   Definition: _____

5. She was a **husky** girl, not small and fragile-looking like her sister.

   Definition: _____

6. Her friends noticed the **spasms** of pain that would periodically shake her body.

   Definition: _____

7. After the leg injury she needed to use a **wheelchair** for six months, so they built a **ramp** beside the stairs so she could get into the house by herself.

   Definitions: _____
   _____

8. The **set** they built for the movie *The Titanic* looked exactly like the inside of the ship.

   Definition: _____

9. I lived for five years at a boarding school that had a special **infirmary** where you were taken if you were really sick.

   Definition: _____

10. Because they hadn't seen each other for a few months, the children spent their first day together acting wild—running around and generally **raising hell**.

    Definition: _____

Follow-Up

The activities in this section will give you a chance to find out more about the topic of this unit and conduct some investigations of your own. You can work on some or all or just one of these activities. There are activities that you can work on alone or with others. You can adapt these activities to meet your needs; you may even think of projects of your own to undertake.

When you study language you often learn about things in life you never knew before.

ACTIVITY NINE   Gathering Information from Reading

Step 1. Read the following questions and think about possible answers. Discuss your ideas with a partner.

1. How do the campers appear to visitors to Hole in the Wall?

2. Why do children go to the infirmary at night?

3. What responsibilities does Sue Johnson have?

4. How are children selected for the camp?

5. How often does Paul Newman visit the camp? What happens when he does?

6. What experience with life-threatening disease have most of the counselors had? What needs do the counselors have?

7. What is the theory behind the Hole in the Wall Gang camp?

8. What has been Dr. Pearson's involvement with the camp since its opening?

9. What can the children learn by being with kids who suffer from diseases other than their own?

10. How many of the children at the camp have cancer? What has been the experience of these children?

11. What is hemophilia? What medical problems do young hemophiliacs have?

12. What goes on at the "Cabin Chat?"

13. What do some children say has been good about having cancer?

14. What do the children say about having to go through cancer treatment?

Step 2. Read the text and locate the sections of the reading that relate to each question. Highlight or underline these sections and mark the question number in the margin. Write your answers in note form.

Step 3. Discuss your answers with a partner or check the answer key.

Hugging Life
by Calvin Trillin

On my first morning at the Hole in the Wall Gang Camp, Joe Frustaci, the woodworking director, stepped up to the dining-hall microphone after breakfast to read a poem that had been written on the back of a wooden heart by Shawn Valdez, a 9-year-old camper who has spent about half his life under treatment for leukemia. The poem was for a counselor named Wendy Whitehill—Shawn's favorite person at the camp, unless you count Tadger, who lives in the woods rather than in the camp itself and may well be a bear.

Shawn—a dark, frail-looking little boy with large brown eyes wasn't facing the microphone. He was sitting on Wendy's lap, with his arms around her neck. What Shawn had written on the heart was:

> Wendy
> I love your golden hair
> Gold as a sunrise
> I love the way you blood
> warms me up like the tow eskimoes
> snuggling.
> I love your smile from
> ear to ear
> I love every
> thing about you
>   Shawn

I met Wendy a few minutes later. Actually, her hair didn't look quite as gold as a sunrise to me, but that may have been because of the light we were in. I said, "Shawn seems to find you an acceptable person."

She smiled and nodded. One of the things that had most struck her about the camp, she said, was the widespread presence of "unconditional love." Partly because all of the campers have been treated for diseases frightening enough to make schoolmates hesitant or even hostile, unconditional love is more or less camp policy. Children hug counselors. Counselors hug children. When Huggy Bear—a bear suit inhabited by an adult, often Robert (Woody) Wilkins, the camp director delivers the mail from Tadger every morning at breakfast, he hugs everybody in sight. When a counselor is sitting down, he is likely to have a camper in his lap.

The Hole in the Wall Gang Camp, which was founded and continues to be energized by the actor Paul Newman, is an unconditional sort of place. It looks like the camp that summer-camp kids have always dreamed of when they were not dreaming of being back in their own beds, just down the hall from their parents—a shrewdly designed, dazzlingly equipped Wild West hideout in eastern Connecticut. The theater resembles the sort of place where dancing girls are about to appear on the stage to be hooted at by rowdies who have just come off a cattle drive. The lake is so well stocked that fish that really want to get caught may have to take a number.

Visitors nearly always remark that the children enjoying the facilities—who range in age from 7 to 15—look sort of, well, normal. The camp is specifically for children with cancer or serious blood disorders; what's wrong with them is on the inside. You might notice a child who is temporarily bald from the effects of chemotherapy or one whose growth has been stunted by the side effects of radiation or one who looks particularly thin; there might be a hemophilic boy (virtually all homophiliacs are boys) who is in a wheelchair because he had a bleed into his spinal cord that couldn't be stopped. Some of the campers tire easily and some were in the hospital when other children their age were developing the hand-eye coordination it takes to look good on the tennis court.

By necessity, the Hole in the Wall Gang Camp is run largely through the infirmary. The closest thing to an admissions director is Sue Johnson, the head nurse, whose pool of applicants is gathered mainly through tertiary-care medical centers. She figures out, for instance, how many hemophiliacs can come to camp in any one session, since the constant need for factor makes them labor-intensive campers. (The diseases themselves impose a certain amount of racial and ethnic balance. Sickle-cell anemia afflicts mainly black people, and sicklers, as they're often called, tend to make up about a tenth of the children at the camp. One of the blood diseases, thalassemia, is so strongly associated with families of Italian and Greek origin that it is sometimes called Mediterranean anemia.) But the infirmary, a rough-wood building in the Western style, is not labeled "The Infirmary"; a sign outside says "The O.K. Corral." Nobody working there wears a white coat. At the camp, medical treatment is supposed to be the engine that doesn't call attention to itself—like the legendary assembly of pipes and cables and computers under Disney World.

Paul Newman thought of the camp as a place where children would be able to escape doctors and hospitals for a while and just be campers. It savors the sort of traditions found in conventional camps. If someone is caught leaving the dining hall through the In door rather than the Out door, for instance, he has to stand in the middle of the dining hall and pantomime the words to the bushy-tail song. When Newman visits the camp—he has built a cabin across the lake, and he's normally around for at least a day or two each 10-day seesion—he always seems to stroll out through the In door, and he is caught by a pack of alert campers every time. Then he has to stand in the middle of the room, doing the appropriate motions, while everyone sings:

> Paul, Paul.
> Shake your bushy tail.
> Shake your bushy tail.
> Wrinkle up your little nose.
> Stick your head between your toes.
> Shake your bushy tail.

As far as I could tell, the only reminder of medicine in the regular camp program is a form of action painting that children in arts and crafts like to do with syringes. Dahlia Lithwick, one of two former counselors who have put together a book of writings by Shawn Valdez and other campers called "I Will Sing Life: Voices From the Hole in the Wall Gang Camp," told me that the older girls in her cabin always spent the conventional amount of time discussing who might be going to the dance with whom. On the other hand, she thinks that campers tend to see their counselors as grown-ups who, unlike parents, don't have to be protected—campers are likely to have spent a lot of time seeing parents with what Shawn's mother calls in the book "tear eyes"—so the question asked a counselor after the dance could be, "I don't want to freak you out, but why do you think God picked me to die?"

The counselor asked such a question will more than likely be freaked out. Although a few of the counselors have had childhood cancer themselves, the camp, which had its first summer in 1988, hasn't been in operation long enough to produce a supply of counselors from former campers. Most of the counselors are college students who have led relatively protected lives, and most of them arrive, in the words of a letter quoted in Newman's introduction for "I Will Sing Life," with "a natural terror of disease, and a couple of books about coping with grief bought in a panic the previous week."

For them, the experience of being at the camp tends to be intense, partly because of the constant juxtaposition of life-threatening illness and problems like who is going to the dance with whom. When Huggy Bear comes through the dining hall, the counselors who jump up to get hugged are partly just joining in, the way they join in the bushy-tail song and the dancing, but some of them may well feel the need of some hugging.

The Hole in the Wall Gang Camp is not, in fact, a camp for dying children. The overwhelming majority of campers, Sue Johnson says, "have a lot to put up with, but they're not terminal." According to Carroll W. Brewster, a former college president who is the executive director of the Hole in the Wall Gang Fund, "the theory is that every child here is going to be an adult and needs a good childhood to become one"— meaning that the camp sees its business as returning to the campers some of the childhood they've lost to illness and treatment.

On the theory that the proper work of childhood is learning and having fun, the camp concentrates on the equivalent of putting the children back to work— teaching horseback riding even if the hemophiliacs have to be given a shot of factor before getting on the horse, for instance, or letting everyone go swimming even if the tendency of sicklers to be thrown into a pain crisis by a chill means that the pool has to be particularly warm and a gazebo next to it is outfitted with heat lamps in the ceiling.

The heated gazebo is known locally as the Pearson French-Fryer Warmer, after Howard A. Pearson, the Yale pediatrician who molded Newman's vision into what became the Hole in the Wall Gang Camp. When Newman was casting around for advice on how to establish a camp in Connecticut for children with cancer, Pearson was the chairman of pediatrics at Yale Medical School and the Yale-New Haven Hospital. His advice seemed to extend naturally into participation. Pearson has been the medical director at the camp from the beginning. He also served for a couple of years as executive director of the Hole in the Wall Gang Fund, which annually raises the $2 million it takes to run a camp that has dazzling equipment but no fees. He's a low-key, grandfatherly man— not the sort of person who finds being a camp doctor beneath the station of an eminent professor who this year is also the president-elect of the American Academy of Pediatrics.

It was Pearson who recommended that children with blood disorders as well as children with cancer be a part of the camp mix. Partly because so much of childhood cancer is leukemia, there has always been a strong overlap in pediatrics between oncology and hematology. Pearson's own research interest is genetic blood disorders. Although the camp now has a couple of special sessions for campers with a single ailment—one for sickle-cell, one for immunological disorders, including HIV infection—Pearson says that a mix is salutary for the general sessions, partly because there is something about any serious disease or its treatment that can make someone with another serious disease count his blessings.

In fact, the camp is one place where a child who has had cancer may have reason to feel in an enviable position, although I suspect that would be a hard proposition to sell to a 10-year-old who's in the middle of an intense course of chemotherapy. The campers who have had a diagnosis of cancer—normally about two-thirds of the 120 children in a regular session—have almost all been through chemotherapy, and some of them have also had surgery and radiation. But the ones who have completed their treatment are likely to lead lives that are not dominated or shortened by disease: the cure rate for the most common type of childhood leukemia is now approaching 80 percent.

That's not true of the sicklers, who are never through with the pain crises and whose bodies tend to give out in their 40's or 50's. Because of considerable progress in recent years in the treatment of hemophilia—mainly the invention of a process to manufacture clotting factor, making constant blood transfusions unnecessary—it appeared for a while that many hemophiliacs would have to face futures of only inconvenience and enormous expense rather than inevitable crippling and early death. But until 1985, the factor supply was not screened for HIV, so about half of the hemophiliacs at the Hole in the Wall Gang Camp are HIV positive.

Although Tadger has never been seen—he is said to be extremely shy—he can be counted on to answer a letter overnight. The campers rarely trouble Tadger with mentions of disease or doctors or hospitals. They tend to tell him that he shouldn't be so shy, or reassure him that they love him, or thank him for the little gifts he sometimes sends. During my stay at the camp, one boy wrote, "I have to tell you that your friend the white bear went out the wrong door, and he had to shake his bushy tail." Hole in the Wall Gang campers aren't embarrassed about mentioning their illness, given the company. "All the kids there have learned to live through things," one of the authors of "I Will Sing Life" wrote about the camp. "We know we're normal people." Apparently, though, the younger children tend not to dwell on the subject—not even in what's called Cabin Chat, a quiet time before bed, when the counselors and the campers talk by the light of a single candle.

I sat in on Cabin Chat one night in a cabin of older boys. Everyone was asked to write down on a piece of paper something, important or trivial, that he would have changed if he'd had the power to change it—the loaded assignment was from a robust-looking counselor who had himself had childhood cancer—and then to toss the paper into a hat. The one piece of paper pulled out said, "Cancer was both the best thing and the worst thing that ever happened to me."

Everyone seemed to agree that the worst thing about having cancer was a drug called prednisone, a steroid that makes some people terribly angry and some people depressed and everybody enormously hungry. A lot of the campers found something good to say about having had cancer, although a certain amount of that had that sound of bravura or rationalization. There was talk about the interesting people they met; a couple of boys mention that cancer enabled them to come to the Hole in the Wall Gang Camp.

A boy who was still undergoing treatment seemed less certain about the good things, but finally he said, "I believe I'm tougher than any other kid in my school, at least mentally."

That led to a discussion about who could make it through cancer treatment and who couldn't. There was considerable feeling that the school bullies, who thought they were so tough, could never make it through.

"No, they'd make it," the toughest boy in his school said. "What choice would they have? Die? We didn't have any choice."

"Hugging Life" by Calvin Trillin, September 6, 1992, Copyright © 1992 by The New York Times Company. Reprinted by permission.

ACTIVITY TEN A Book Report

As you heard in the program, the writings of some of the campers appear in the book *I Will Sing Life: Voices from the Hole in the Wall Gang Camp,* published by Little, Brown & Co. In this activity you will have an opportunity to read these writings and to write a report on your thoughts about the book. To carry out this activity you can

1. Read the book (take five to seven days to complete the reading).

2. Choose a section of the book that most interested you (perhaps the essay of one individual author, or a few short selections by several authors).

3. Write your reactions to these writings in your journal. You can do this over the course of several days. You do not have to worry about sentence structure or grammatical correctness; just write ideas as they come to you. You may want to discuss your thoughts with others in class.

4. At the end of the week of reading and writing reactions, read over what you have written and prepare a first draft of your book report.

5. Your report should explain the section of the book you chose, how it reflects the content of the book as a whole, your reaction to the content and emotion of the writing, and whether or not you would recommend the book to others.

6. The day after writing your first draft, reread what you wrote and make any changes you think are necessary.

7. Write your final draft and then submit it to your teacher.

SUGGESTIONS FOR OTHER FOLLOW-UP ACTIVITIES

Speaking: Group Activities/Individual Activities
Role-play:

Take the role of one of the Hole in the Wall Gang summer campers. Prepare a short monologue about your experiences at camp, describing how these experiences have affected you. You can tape or orally present your monologue.

Writing: Individual Activities
Summary of "Summer Camp for Sick Kids"
Personal reaction to the story of Pia

Listening: Individual/Group Activities
At home: Listening to TV or radio broadcasts
  (See pp. 18–19 for de-tails about this activity.)
Attend a local book launching or artists' reading.

Tiny Survivors: Saving Preemies

4

OVERVIEW

Preparing to Listen

Activity One	Discussion Questions
Activity Two	Examining the Data: Comparing Developmental Stages
Activity Three	Predictions; Bridge to Listening

Listening to the Tape

Activity Four	Listening for the Main Ideas
Activity Five	Writing Focused Notes
Activity Six	Comprehension Questions

Language Close Up

Activity Seven	Language Focus: Verbs
Activity Eight	Language Focus: Roots, Prefixes, and Suffixes
Activity Nine	Vocabulary: Guessing Meaning from Context

Follow-Up

Activity Ten	Gathering Information from Reading; Retells

In North America there has been an increase in both the percentage of babies born prematurely and in the percentage of those tiny babies who are able to survive. Medical technology is saving the lives of children who were once at risk if they were born before term. In this program you will hear from the parents and physicians who care for these prematurely born babies. The activities will help you to understand and use the information you listen to.

Preparing to Listen

Getting some background information and thinking about the topic before you hear the program will help you to understand the ideas more easily. Complete the activities in this section **before you listen.**

ACTIVITY ONE Discussion Questions

What do you think? Read and consider the following questions. Write your ideas in note form and discuss them with others.

1. How many weeks do women normally carry a baby before it is born? At what point in the pregnancy can a baby be born prematurely and still survive?

2. Why are babies born prematurely?

3. What are the dangers of premature birth to the mother and the baby?

4. How has medical technology improved the chances for survival of premature babies? What kind of care can we give today that we couldn't give a few decades ago?

5. What are the present limits to what technology can or should do for these babies? What are the consequences of saving preemies?

ACTIVITY TWO Examining the Data: Comparing Developmental Stages

It is now possible to save some babies who are born as many as four months before they are due. Look at the developmental chart and examine the charac-

Pushing Back the Edge of the Envelope

Medical research has extended the age of viability for premature babies to 24 weeks—16 weeks short of a normal full-term baby. The chart below illustrates the developmental range of newborns hospitals can save today: from tiny 24-weekers who must be artificially sustained to chubby, seven-pound 40-weekers.

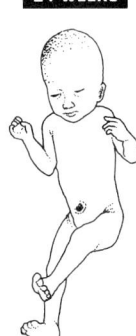

24 WEEKS
Height: 13 inches
Weight: 1¼ pounds
Lungs just developed enough for mechanical ventilation. All babies have dark red appearance because skin pigmentation has not begun. Skin is unable to help regulate body temperature or ward off infection. Eyes are often fused shut, ear lobes just skin flaps. Baby has 5-20 percent chance of survival outside the womb.

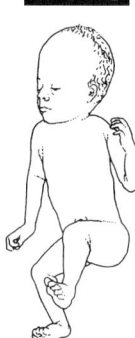

29 WEEKS
Height: 14½ inches
Weight: 2½ pounds
Lungs have developed enough to increase chances of survival outside womb to 90-95 percent. Baby takes on a more rounded, plump appearance because fat layer is developing. Pigmentation is present. Eyes partly open. Baby can follow objects with its eyes and has longer periods of alertness. Some babies begin to suck.

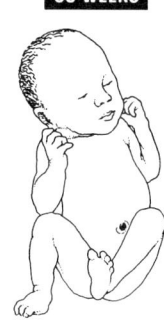

35 WEEKS
Height: 18½ inches
Weight: 5½ pounds
Baby sees almost as well as a full-term baby and shows a preference for a human face. Testicles in the male have descended. Baby can coordinate sucking, breathing and swallowing to allow nipple feeding. Skin is smooth because of substantial fat layer. Muscle tone so well developed that heel can no longer touch ear.

40 WEEKS
Height: 20 inches
Weight: 7 pounds
Baby plump and fully developed. Baby has received iron, calcium, vitamins and immunities against infection from mother.

Newsweek 5/16/88, Lewis Calver.

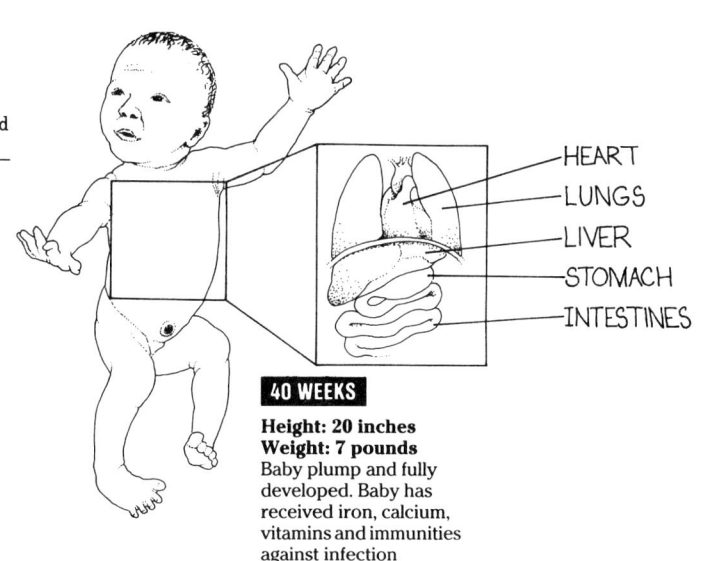

teristics of premature babies at various stages of development. Scan the information and find the answers to the following questions:

1. How much weight does a baby gain between the 24th and 40th week of development?

2. How much does the baby gain in height between the 24th and 40th week?

58 △ Tiny Survivors: Saving Preemies

3. Compare the odds of survival outside the womb for babies at 24 weeks and babies at 29 weeks.

_____

_____

4. Compare the eye development of babies at 24, 29, and 35 weeks.

_____

_____

5. What is the skin of a baby at 24 weeks unable to do? How does the skin change as the baby develops?

_____

_____

Discuss your answers with a partner or check the answer key.

ACTIVITY THREE Predictions; Bridge to Listening

Part One: Predictions

Based on what you know or expect to know about the subject, what information do you think this program will present?

Write your ideas on the lines below. You can write your ideas in either words or phrases, in question or sentence form. Write any ideas you have. Don't worry about whether they are good or bad or whether they are correctly written.

1. _____
2. _____
3. _____
4. _____

Discuss your predictions. Later, you can check to see what you were able to predict accurately.

Part Two: Bridge to Listening

The purpose of the introduction is to prepare you for the information in the program. It can give you an overview or a taste of something interesting to come.

Step 1. Cue your tape to the introduction of the show, which begins, "Worldwide, a large number of babies." Turn on your tape.

Step 2. Listen to the introduction, which ends, "that story from Los Angeles, California," without stopping the tape. Think about the information as you listen. Stop the tape at the end of the introduction.

Step 3. Write two or three important ideas in note form.
The first is given as an example.

1. premature babies = pre/37–40 wks./not full-pregnancy
2.
3.

Discuss your ideas with a partner or check the answer key. Compare these ideas to the predictions you made before.

Listening to the Tape

The activities in this section will help you to practice your skills in understanding and using the information you hear. Concentrate on the task you have to accomplish and practice the skills (for example, note taking) needed to complete the task. Remember the strategies for coping with listening to radio reports listed on page 5:

- Focus on what you understand.
- Don't worry about information that goes by quickly.
- Share information and clarify what you're not sure of.

Note Taking

In many of the activities that follow you will be identifying the main ideas and supporting points and details and often writing what you hear in note form. These activities will help you get more of the important information in your notes more quickly.

For a few tips about writing quick notes as you listen, read the information on page 6. For more complete information about improving your note taking skills, refer to the Guide to Note Taking (Appendix 1, p. 93).

ACTIVITY FOUR — Listening for the Main Ideas

Step 1. Listen to the program "Tiny Survivors: Saving Preemies" without stopping. Number the following main ideas according to the order in which you hear them.

( ) **A.** Breakthroughs in preventing lung disease

( ) **B.** Preventing pre-term births

( ) **C.** Machinery used to keep preemies alive

( ) **D.** The experience of Shirley Jordan

Step 2. Discuss your answers with a partner or check the answer key.

ACTIVITY FIVE — Writing Focused Notes

When you listen to a radio report you hear a wonderful mix of voices and sounds. The information that you hear is a mixture of factual information blended with opinion and emotion. A radio report isn't always organized in the same logical pattern as a good academic lecture. It follows a pattern of describing or explaining the important ideas (main points and details) related to the topic, from the reporter's point of view.

Your task is to listen and take notes so that you will be able to explain the main points and important details of this report to someone who has questions about advances in saving the lives of premature babies. The focused notes you write for the general questions will help you to discuss the details of what you heard with others.

DIRECTIONS To take focused notes follow these steps:

Step 1. Read the following general questions and think about the information you heard. What details relating to each question can you recall?

1. What happened to Shirley Jordan? How did she feel?
2. What problems do premature babies have?
3. What new machinery is being used in intensive care units? How does it help premature babies?
4. What lung problems did babies have in the past? How are these problems treated today?
5. What does Shirley think of her son's progress? What do doctors hope for?

Step 2. If possible, discuss these questions with others.

Step 3. Rewind to the beginning of the program. Start the tape. As you listen, write details in note form for each of the questions you have just read or discussed. If necessary, take notes on a separate sheet of paper.

Read the sample notes to see what kind of detail is important and how to write in note form. Try taking notes yourself as you listen to the tape. Compare what you have written to the sample notes provided. Your wording may not be the same, but the ideas should be.

1. What happened to Shirley Jordan? How did she feel?

    -Labor/2 mnths early
    -funny
    -not sure how to feel

2. What problems do premature babies have?

3. What new machinery is being used in intensive care units? How does it help premature babies?

4. What lung problems did babies have in the past? How are these problems treated today?

5. What does Shirley think of her son's progress? What do doctors hope for?

Step 4. Stop the tape at the end of the program. Read over your notes. If you have a partner, discuss what you heard and wrote. As you read or discuss, add information to your notes.

Step 5 (Optional). Listen another time to confirm and complete your notes. Read your notes and discuss again.

ACTIVITY SIX   Comprehension Questions

Answering these questions correctly is a check on the accuracy of your listening.

Step 1. Read the following questions and use your notes to answer as many questions as possible. Write the answers to these questions **in note form.**

The first question is done as an example.

1. When and where did Shirley Jordan go into labor? How did she react?

    7 mnths pregnant, friend's house, surprised, disbelief

2. What was Shirley's baby like at birth? What is he like now?

3. In what area of neonatology have doctors made little progress?

4. What is the biggest killer of premature babies?

5. What kind of nursery is the PICU at Kaiser Hospital in Hollywood?

6. What is an incubator and what does it do for a baby?

7. What is the high-frequency ventilator?

8. What does this ventilator do?

9. What have the doctors attached to the foot of the baby hooked up to the ventilator? What are the function and advantages of this device?

10. Can parents touch their babies?

11. What does surfactant enable the lungs to do? Why is surfactant production a problem for preemies?

12. How have doctors solved the problem of preemies' lack of surfactant?

13. What do such medical breakthroughs make possible?

14. What does Shirley Jordan think of her son?

15. What do doctors hope to be able to do in the future?

Step 2. Discuss the information with others.

Step 3 (Optional). If you need to, listen to the program to find answers that you don't have or can't agree on. Stop the tape when you hear the information you are listening for and write your answer.

Language Close Up

In this section you can practice listening for specific language. The activities focus on different features, such as improving your awareness of grammatical form or improving your ability to hear key details. The activities will help you to be more aware of the different tones, colloquial expressions, and speaking styles people use when they talk. You can learn vocabulary through the practice of guessing meaning from context.

ACTIVITY SEVEN — Language Focus: Verbs

In this program you heard people talking about their experiences and explaining the technical side of their work. Noticing the choice of verb, its tense, and voice is useful in understanding this part of the story.

Before listening, read and complete any of the missing information you can remember from the partial transcript that follows. Then, listen to the tape of the segment and complete as much as you can.

Cue to the beginning of this segment.

"We _____ _____ at my girlfriend's house, and we _____ _____ our baby shower. And I _____ something _____ funny, but I _____ _____ sure because I _____ in my seventh month, or just getting into the seventh month, and I _____ sure how I _____ _____ _____ _____ at this point."

But it _____ _____ and Shirley Jordan _____ birth nearly two months early to a four-pound, three-ounce boy. But today's technology _____ his chance for survival high. In fact, little Jordan Schaeffer, who _____ now a healthy, thriving toddler, _____ home with his parents just ten days after his premature birth.

Read over and complete the segment you heard. If you need to, listen again. If you are working in pairs, read the segment to your partner. If you are working alone, check your work with the transcript. You can read the segment along with your tape.

ACTIVITY EIGHT — Language Focus: Roots, Prefixes, and Suffixes

In this program you heard a number of words that are specifically related to the topic. As is often the case, the meaning of these words can be guessed if you know a little about the subject. But knowing the meaning or function of one

64   Tiny Survivors: Saving Preemies

part of the word—the beginning (prefix) or the ending (suffix)—can help you guess the meaning of the whole word.

Step 1. Before listening, read and complete any of the missing information you can remember from the partial transcript that follows. Then, listen to the tape of the segment and complete as much as you can.

Doctor Myron Bethel is an _____ at the Hospital of the Good Samaritan in Los Angeles. He says, while there have been significant _____ in keeping _____ babies alive, there's been little _____ in lowering the number of _____ births.

"I don't think we've gotten any better at _____ _____ labor or—I.D.'ing those _____ at risk. We have just the _____ _____ we give them to _____ the amount of work, and _____ _____ to stress, _____ _____ _____ and relative rest is the only thing we can offer.

Read over and complete the segment you heard. If you need to, listen again. If you have a partner, read these segments to each other. If you are working alone, play the tape again and read the segments along with your tape.

Step 2. Finding the Roots

List the words you filled in to complete the segment. For each word, give the root, the prefix or suffix, the meaning of the word part, and the meaning of the word itself. Find another word that has the same prefix, suffix, or root and give its meaning.

Use a dictionary to complete this task.

(FIND THE MEANING FOR EACH)

	Word	Root	Prefix	Suffix	Meaning	New Word & Meaning
1.	_____	_____	_____	_____	_____	_____
2.	_____	_____	_____	_____	_____	_____
3.	_____	_____	_____	_____	_____	_____
4.	_____	_____	_____	_____	_____	_____
5.	_____	_____	_____	_____	_____	_____
6.	_____	_____	_____	_____	_____	_____
7.	_____	_____	_____	_____	_____	_____

(FIND THE MEANING FOR EACH)

Word	Root	Prefix	Suffix	Meaning	New Word & Meaning
8.					
9.					
10.					
11.					
12.					
13.					
14.					
15.					

Discuss your answers with a partner or check the answer key.

ACTIVITY NINE Vocabulary: Guessing Meaning from Context

You heard the words **in bold print** in the program. In this activity you will focus on the language used and guess the meaning of these words from the context in which they are used.

Step 1. Read each sentence. Based on your understanding of the sentence, try to guess what the word or words mean.

Step 2. Write your own definition for the words in bold print. You can check your definition with a partner or consult your dictionary.

1. When Ann realized that she **was in labor** with her first baby, she was very excited, but nervous because she wasn't sure how difficult giving birth would be.

   Definition: _____

2. When Susan was seven months pregnant her sister decided to organize a **baby shower.** She invited friends and relatives to the party and suggested presents they could bring for the baby.

   Definition: _____

3. The baby was born at seven months of **gestation,** or six weeks before the **due date,** and weighed only four pounds and three ounces, which is about two kilos.

   Definitions: _____
   _____

4. The playground, which was specially designed to be safe for **toddlers,** was filled with two-year-olds having a great time.

   Definition: _____

5. It is very common for large companies to sponsor programs on stress management for their employees who work in high-pressure jobs to reduce the risk of **occupational exposure** to stress.

   Definition: _____

6. The speaker delivered his talk so quickly that I wondered how he expected us to take it all in; we just couldn't **absorb** it all.

   Definition:_____

7. We worked all week to produce a good general model for the manufacturer; now we only have to **fine-tune** the details of the design.

   Definition:_____

8. Eye surgery used to require a lot of **invasive** procedures—cutting, removing tissue with a scalpel, and sewing. Now, with lasers, the eye can be repaired without that kind of damage.

   Definition:_____

9. The children were **squirting** water at each other and everyone got wet.

   Definition:_____

10. We all started out on the walk together, but after an hour some people slowed down and started to **lag** behind.

    Definition:_____

Follow-Up

The activities in this section will give you a chance to find out more about the topic of this unit and conduct some investigations of your own. You can work on some or all or just one of these activities. There are activities that you can work on alone or with others. You can adapt these activities to meet your needs; you may even think of projects of your own to undertake.

When you study language you often learn about things in life you never knew before.

ACTIVITY TEN   Gathering Information from Reading; Retells

Part One: Finding the Main Ideas

Step 1. Preview the text. Quickly read all of the introduction, which ends after the third complete paragraph with the words, "has become more of a burden than a blessing." Read the first and last sentence of all the other paragraphs. Read all of the conclusion, which begins at the section "Quiet moment." What is the general theme of the article? Write the theme in your own words and discuss what you wrote with a partner.

Theme: _____

_____

Preemies
Barbara Kantrowitz with Pat Wingert and Mary Hager

On the morning of January 7, as Jewel McNeill's labor pains grew stronger and stronger, a nurse came into the delivery room. Did the NcNeills have any plans for burying their baby? she asked grimly. Would they want an autopsy? Jewel recalls her using the phrase "disposing of the fetus." Her husband, Michael, noticed a receptacle that looked like a trash can at the bottom of the table. This, he thought, would be his baby's only cradle. According to the hospital's calculations, Jewel was no more than 22 weeks pregnant—18 weeks short of full term. The baby would weigh barely a pound and its lungs would be too undeveloped to sustain life. The doctor told Jewel to start pushing. Better to end the agony. A few minutes later, at exactly 10:08 a.m., Briana Adia-Jewel McNeill was born.

Alive.

Her eyes were open, her arms and legs were wiggling and she began to cry. To Jewel, it sounded like a cry for help.

If Briana had been born 10 or even five years ago, her cry might have gone unanswered. Doctors could not resolve the multiple problems of babies born so small and so young. Lung disease, hemorrhaging, infection—the list of potential killers was too long. Throughout the 1970s, premature babies more than twice her size faced slim odds of survival. But progress was on Briana's side. In the last few years, doctors have made tremendous advances in the practice of neonatology (the care of newborn babies). With the aid of sophisticated medical equipment and newly developed techniques, they are able to save babies so small that they fit in an adult's palm.

By early afternoon on Jan. 7, Briana had been transferred to the Intensive Care Nursery (ICN) at Georgetown University Hospital in Washington, D.C., a short distance away from the hospital where she was born. There, amidst a blaze of lights and the constant peal of alarms, the sickest and tiniest of babies struggle for another day of life. The cost is high—in human as well as financial terms. Although the vast majority of premature babies will live normal lives, others will die after days or weeks of round-the-clock care. And a few will survive with disabilities so severe that their parents will wonder if the technology that saved their babies has become more of a burden than a blessing.

The most troubled babies are born at the current limit of viability, about 24 weeks old with a weight of about 500 grams (just over a pound). They bear little resemblance to full-term newborns. Their ear lobes are often just skin flaps at the sides of their heads and their eyes may be fused shut. Their skin is a dusky red color no matter what their race; normal pigmentation comes about a month later. Their lungs have developed to the point where they can breathe with the help of a machine called a ventilator; the lungs of babies any younger than this are so rudimentary that the infants have virtually no chance of survival.

Neonatologists say that it is lung development that puts these babies on the edge of survival; the next goal for researchers may be to come up with a substitute for the oxygenation of blood in the womb; no one knows when or if that will happen. In the meantime, doctors use the knowledge they gain by saving the smallest babies to increase the odds for older preemies.

According to one recent government survey, about 17,000 infants weighing less than about two pounds are admitted annually to about 420 ICN's around the country. They currently have about a 70 percent chance of survival. Larger babies do better. Ninety percent of infants weighing from about two to three pounds live; in the early 1960s, more than half of them died.

Preemies—technically any baby born more than three weeks early—make up only about 10 percent of the annual live births in this country, but the cost of their care can be astronomical. In the more sophisticated hospitals, those most likely to have ICN's, bills can add up to hundreds of thousands of dollars for the very tiny babies. And that may not be the end of it. A sizable percentage of very small preemies wind up with moderate to severe handicaps that may need treatment for years.

Newborn care: Preemies represent a disproportionate amount of the money spent on newborn care, says Rachel Schwartz, associate director of the National Perinatal Information Center in Providence, R.I. In 1985, the most recent year for which such figures are available, $1.9 billion was spent on babies born in the most advanced hospitals. Of that, 62 percent—about $1.2 billion—went to care for only 11.1 percent of the cases, babies born weighing less than 2,500 grams (about five pounds).

The sums are huge, but they are far smaller than money spent for other forms of health care. In 1985, for example, $5 billion was spent for all newborn care in hospitals, compared with $72.3 billion for all Medicare expenditures.

Every day in the ICN, doctors, nurses and parents struggle with unanswerable questions. Is it right to continue aggressive treatment for infants who may not have much of a chance at normal life? And who should decide what is an acceptable quality of life? Should such extensive financial and technological resources be devoted to a relatively few patients? Wouldn't the money be better spent providing prenatal care and thus preventing many premature births?

And—perhaps most troubling of all—if it is possible to save babies at 24 weeks, then how can we justify legal abortions at that point? Has medicine outpaced law? Progress in the nursery is forcing us to confront basic issues. "Science and technology don't have the power to tell us when life begins," says Arthur Kaplan of the Center for Biomedical Ethics at the University of Minnesota. "What they do have is the power to give us information and evidence which we must reckon with as we try to draw lines between life and death, fetus and person, mother's rights and baby's rights."

Drawing those boundaries is easy when a preemie on the edge of life grows into a healthy baby. Briana McNeill was one of the lucky ones. At Georgetown, doctors examined her and revised the original estimate of her age. They said she had been in her mother's womb between 24 and 25 weeks. She weighed 560 grams—about one pound, four ounces. That gave her about a 20 percent chance of survival, according to Dr. K. N. Siva Subramanian, Georgetown's chief of neonatology. Over the next three and a half months, a team of highly trained doctors and nurses monitored her every heartbeat and breath for signs of trouble. Unlike most of the babies in the ICN, Briana had no serious setbacks. On April 20 Jewel and Michael took her home. By last week she weighed more than five pounds and was doing well.

Slow death: But what about the babies who don't do well? Is the struggle worth it for them? Jewel McNeill remembers another mother, whose premature baby was in the ICN as Jewel prepared to take Briana home. His condition was rapidly deteriorating. There were more than half a dozen tubes and wires inserted in various parts of his body, and his skin was a mottled purple. He was breathing through a special ventilator that made his body shake constantly. Jewel tried to comfort the mother, but the woman could not be consoled; the doctors had already told her that her baby would not make it through the week.

On the morning that Jewel came in to get Briana, she looked around for the other mother. A nurse told her the boy had died. "I burst into tears," Jewel said. "Here I am going home and I'm crying. It's so hard to be happy. You can't help but feel for someone else. I was almost there myself."

ICN doctors live with uncertainty. "You simply cannot tell early on which babies are going to make it and which are not," says Laurence McCullough, a professor of community medicine at Georgetown. If a baby has no obvious life-threatening defects that cannot be fixed, doctors almost always begin treatment. Many doctors feel they have not only a moral but also a legal obligation to treat the vast majority of preemies because of the so-called "Baby Doe" rules—federal regulations that prohibit withholding treatment unless a child is dying. Once treatment begins, there are no guarantees, only probabilities. Even babies who are doing well can suddenly take a turn for the worse. Siva tells parents that a preemie's journey through the ICN is a little like negotiating an obstacle course in the dark. You may get over one hurdle but there's no way of knowing if more—or bigger—hurdles lie ahead.

'Decision points': Because each infant presents unique problems, there's no set approach to treatment. "We have to go baby by baby, judging by what we see," says Dr. Roderic Phibbs of the University of California at San Francisco. "There are decision points all along the way." Many factors, aside from weight and age, are considered in evaluating an infant's chances for survival. Sex and race are important. Phibbs says that black girls do best; white boys are least likely to make it.

A preemie's first hours are crucial. If they are born in a hospital with an ICN, preemies generally do better, because they are closer to help. Special transport teams bring in babies from other hospitals. The ICN staff evaluates each new baby, checking every vital sign frequently. The newest and sickest babies are usually out in the open under special warmers so the staff has easy access. Hooking up the wires and tubes that form their substitute womb is a painstaking task. Sometimes the nurses or doctors will try two or three times before they get it right.

There are no lullabies in this nursery, just an incessant chorus of alarms. Most of the time, the alarms mean that a baby's oxygen or blood gas level has reached a point where it has to be checked. But if there is a real emergency, the staff quickly gathers around a baby, each person doing a specific job. There can be more than half a dozen people hovering over a tiny patient—doctors, nurses, respiratory therapists or X-ray technicians. The staff is surprisingly quiet during the moments of greatest drama. Often, as a nurse sticks yet another needle into an infant, she whispers softly: "I'm so sorry, baby. So sorry."

Every once in a while, there is an unusual noise that makes everyone stop and look up. It is the sound of a baby crying. Most of the babies are either too weak to cry or are attached to machines that prevent them from making any noise. The staff must guess what the babies are feeling by reading monitors. An increase in blood pressure or heart rate—those are the ICN's equivalent of a baby's cry.

Line of defense: Georgetown's ICN has room for 18 babies. There are another 14 beds in the intermediate-care nursery across the hall. Babies are sent there when they no longer need constant attention. In the ICN, the nurses, who work 12-hour shifts with few breaks, care for no more than two at a time. Extremely ill babies sometimes have two nurses at their side. The nurses are the first line of defense and have the most intimate contact with the infants. They are constantly recording the babies' vital signs and checking for indications of infection. Not even a disposable diaper is thrown away without examination.

The smallest and sickest babies are fed intravenously; a mixture of medicine and food is slowly squeezed through a large syringe into a long tube that enters the baby through a catheter or an i.v. needle. But the nurses provide more than physical nourishment. They make up nicknames for their wards and caress them gently as they treat them. When a baby dies, they grieve; the antidote is to remember the babies who make it. Their pictures fill a row of bulletin boards in the hallway outside the ICN.

The stress of the job is great, and turnover rates for nurses in ICN's are high. Janet Vail, who supervises the 64 nurses who work in Georgetown's ICN and intermediate-care nursery, says there is an average annual attrition rate of 27 percent. The best way to combat the stress, she says, is to have friends outside of the hospital. "Your world here becomes the world of sick babies," she says. "If you only live and breathe the nursery, you will slowly go mad."

'Raw field': There is an eerie sense of isolation inside the ICN. Siva says that when a new unit was built a few years ago, he insisted that it have windows so the staff would always be able to see that there was a real world outside. But even on a fine spring day, when the windows offer a glimpse of flowering trees, the ICN imposes its own reality on everyone inside. Some of the nurses say the place, with all the lights and incessant noise, reminds them of a spaceship. Other staff members say they feel they are on a frontier. That's the image Siva had when he first entered an ICN during his medical training nearly two decades ago. "It was a raw field," he says, "that was ready to explode, just like the West."

Indeed, most of the great advances in neonatology have taken place in the last 20 years. Until very recently, doctors left preemies pretty much alone after they were born. They were fed and cared for, but there was no aggressive treatment. According to the conventional wisdom, "the best thing to do was nothing," says Dr. Ronald Poland, head of neonatology at Detroit's Children's Hospital. "What turned it around," he says, "were zealous people who decided to make a career of finding out what was wrong with these babies and how they could be made to live."

Dr. Charlotte Catz of the National Institute of Child Health and Human Development says that while determination played a vital role, advances in technology were also crucial. Molded plastic incubators enabled doctors to watch the babies from all sides; early models were made of wood with just a small glass window for viewing. Miniaturization of equipment was another major step, along with the development to computers that made continuous monitoring possible. These advances coincided with a growing interest in newborn physiology, especially the physiology of lung function.

One of the very first ICN's was started 27 years ago at Vanderbilt Medical Center in Nashville, Tenn. It was part of a research project headed by Dr. Mildred Stahlman, now the director of Vanderbilt's neonatal program. As other hospitals around the country began to set up their own ICN's throughout the 1960s and 1970s, techniques were adapted from adult medicine. For the first 10 years, the new units had little success with babies under 1,500 grams—about 3 pounds, 5 ounces. Respiratory failure was the most frequent cause of death.

At each stage there were new obstacles. In the early years, preemies were given pure oxygen to breathe. Although their survival rate improved, many had an eye disease called retrolental fibroplasia that often caused blindness. Researchers pinpointed too much oxygen as a culprit. Blindness declined as oxygen use dropped, but more babies died. Finally, doctors developed methods for monitoring oxygen levels, reducing both blindness and deaths.

Tiny lungs: Lung failure was another cause of fatalities. The death rate from the condition known as hyaline membrane disease, or respiratory distress syndrome, was 90 percent. In the early 1960s, doctors discovered that a substance known as surfactant provides surface tension in the lungs' air sacs. Natural surfactant had not developed in many preemies; without it, the tiny air sacs would collapse and stick together with every breath, the cause of respiratory distress. The infants' tiny lungs had to be expanded and contracted mechanically by a ventilator. As ventilator use grew, more babies lived. But again, there are side effects. Some infants' fragile lungs are damaged by the ventilator and they develop chronic lung disease. Others become ventilator-dependent. Researchers are now working on methods of injecting natural or artificial surfactant into babies' lungs.

Brain hemorrhages continue to be a major problem. Serious bleeding and lack of blood supply to the brain lead to severe brain damage; in other cases, infants have cerebral palsy or are spastic. Blindness is also on the increase again. The victims are the very smallest babies. Doctors are trying to figure out why some babies are affected and others aren't.

Despite the advances, doctors have much to learn about what goes on inside the womb. Even with the best of care in the ICN, "Mother Nature does it better," says Dr. Joseph Warshaw of Yale Medical School. "A lot of what we do is trying to catch up." Some things can't be reproduced, such as the amount of calcium a fetus gets from the mother. As a result, very premature babies have brittle bones that break easily. The infants have no ability to control body temperature. Their skin is like gelatin, not a good barrier to infection or water loss.

High risk: Some doctors think the best approach is to concentrate on causes rather than effects. "I have a lot of respect for the neonatologists," says Dr. Michael Katz, an obstetrician at the University of California at San Francisco, "but they are putting out the fire instead of preventing it." Yet even if all high-risk mothers could be identified and treated, prematurity would not be totally eliminated. No one really understands what triggers ordinary labor, much less premature labor.

Researchers are also studying preemies' long-term prospects. The two most important factors appear to be how sick the babies were and their home environment. After following a group of preemies into their school years, University of California psychologist Jane Hunt found that nearly a third were functioning normally, another half had relatively minor problems and the rest had moderate to severe disabilities. Preemies most likely to have serious problems in later life were those who had been very ill at birth and whose families had low educational levels.

Many experts feel parents need help that extends long beyond the ICN. "We need to spend more money on follow up for those who do survive," says Daniel Callahan, director of the Hastings Center, a think tank on biomedical issues. "We should try to keep from pushing the limits and work with what we have." Some hospitals are providing that support. New York's Columbia-Presbyterian Medical Center has a program that tracks the course of its ICN babies in an effort to catch problems early on so that a baby can get proper treatment. Other children follow a different course. As medical director of the Hospital for Sick Children in Washington, D.C., Dr. Constance Battle says she is "immersed in the tragic outcomes of well-intentioned treatment." The children in her hospital are sent there because they are not sick enough for intensive care but are too sick to go home. Many are dependent on ventilators; others have serious handicaps. She has some advice for the neonatologists: "I say give it some thought when you whip something into life you never see again. You don't understand the limbo the child lives in."

Even when parents are able to bring their children home, they find that raising a child with severe disabilities can be emotionally and financially draining—and the strain is even greater when it is piled on top of what may have been months of following a baby's rocky course in the ICN. "Society is not helping parents of the disabled child," says Ernlé W. D. Young, an ethicist at Stanford Medical School. Debbie and Bill Lonstein's daughter Joan was born 15 weeks prematurely last Nov. 13. During her four months in Georgetown's ICN, she suffered the most serious degree of brain hemorrhaging, and her lungs were badly damaged. Joan is home now, but the uncertainty continues. She may have severe brain damage and cerebral palsy. She may never be able to swallow or suck. "When I hold her in my arms, she's my baby and I want her to live," says Debbie. "We appreciate every day we have with her, but sometimes you can't help but wonder whether this is the best for her. We don't know that she'll ever be able to enjoy her life, that she'll ever see the sun and the sky."

Her husband adds: "There was a time when we were afraid she would die. Now there are times when we're afraid she'll live. Without this technology, she would have died naturally, and we wouldn't have had to ask ourselves these questions. Maybe that would have been better."

Quiet moment: For every troubling story like the Lonsteins' there are dozens of successes—and that is what the ICN staffs try to remember. One night recently, during a quiet moment in the unit, several nurses at Georgetown talked about the babies who made it and the ones who didn't. There was one boy they all recalled because he had taught them a lesson about the limits of their craft. In his four months in the unit, he underwent just about every major procedure. There were terrible setbacks, all kinds of infections, moments that everyone thought would signal the end. But the baby just kept fighting, and he went home a few weeks after the day he was supposed to be born.

"Babies like that, I think they do it just to spite us all, to show us that we don't know everything," said Karen Turner.

"No," said Elizabeth Joyal, in a soft voice. "They do it just to give us hope." *Kantrowitz, "Preemies" from Newsweek 5/16/88. 1988, Newsweek, Inc. All rights reserved. Reprinted by permission.*

Step 2. Reread the article and highlight the main ideas. Write a list of six main ideas explained or issues raised in this article.

A. _____
B. _____
C. _____
D. _____
E. _____
F. _____

Discuss your ideas with a partner or check the answer key.

Part Two: Note Taking; Retelling

Note Taking

Step 3. Choose one or two of the main ideas explained in the article. Make notes on the supporting points and details related to the idea(s) you chose. To carry out this task use a divided-page note taking form like the following:

Main Ideas	Supporting Pts./Details

Step 4. In discussion with a partner who made notes for the same information you did, compare your supporting points and details. Change and complete your notes as needed.

Retelling

Step 5 (Optional). Practice telling your information to a partner who prepared notes for the same ideas.

Step 6. Exchange information with partners who prepared notes for different ideas.

For further discussion:

Think about the following questions and share your ideas with others.

1. What kind of support needs to be given to expectant mothers and parents of premature babies?

2. What kinds of problems can we expect to see in the future as more and more premature babies survive? Are we risking an increase in the number of handicapped or disabled children?
3. Should doctors do everything they can to save the life of a premature baby, regardless of its chances of survival?
4. Who should decide whether or not to continue aggressive treatment for a preemie?
5. Are there limits to our ability to afford the cost of saving premature babies and providing for their medical care?

SUGGESTIONS FOR OTHER FOLLOW-UP ACTIVITIES

Speaking: Group Activities

- Debate or panel discussion:
  Should We Continue to Extend Our Capacity to Save Preemies, Regardless of Cost?
- Problem-solving task:
  Given a fixed hospital budget, determine priorities for funding research and equipment for different departments.

Individual Activities

- Three-minute talk:
  Prepare a speech that focuses on the importance of improving preemies' chances of survival. Consider playing a role in making your presentation—the role of a parent or, perhaps, doctor, or of an adult who was born prematurely. You may tape or orally present your talk.

Writing: Individual Activities

- Summary of "Tiny Survivors: Saving Preemies."
- Expository essay:
  "The Reasons We Must Continue to Make Advances in Saving Premature Babies"

Listening: Individual/Group Activities

- Invite someone to speak on a health topic to your class or attend a lecture on health care issues.
- Using your skills at home:
  Listen to a health broadcast related to the topic of this program—life-saving advances in medical procedure and technology. Choose a TV or radio news show or documentary report. See pages 18–19 for details about this activity.

Top Dogs in Detroit: Eyes for the Unsighted

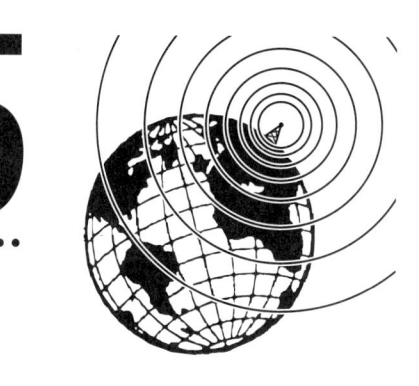

5

OVERVIEW

Preparing to Listen

Activity One	Getting Information from Illustrations
Activity Two	Reading Retell; Fact Gathering for Discussion
Activity Three	Predictions; Bridge to Listening

Listening to the Tape

Activity Four	Listening for the Main Ideas
Activity Five	Writing Focused Notes
Activity Six	Comprehension Questions

Language Close Up

| Activity Seven | Language Focus: Asking and Answering Questions |
| Activity Eight | Vocabulary: Guessing Meaning from Context |

Follow-Up

| Activity Nine | Scanning for Information from a Pamphlet; Reading Retells |
| Activity Ten | Self-Evaluation |

Top Dogs in Detroit: Eyes for the Unsighted

People who do not have the use of their eyes face constant challenges in daily life. One of these is to move around independently out in the world. This program brings you up close to look at a special program in the United States that successfully offers this opportunity to the unsighted. The activities will help you to understand and use the information you listen to.

Preparing to Listen

Getting some background information and thinking about the topic before you hear the program will help you to understand the ideas more easily. Complete the activities in this section **before you listen.**

ACTIVITY ONE

Getting Information from Illustrations

DIRECTIONS

Step 1. Choose one of the pictures and study it carefully. Look at the action shown in the illustration.

Step 2. Prepare an oral description explaining what the picture shows, as well as the thoughts and emotions of the people involved and the sounds they might be hearing. Include as much as you can.

Step 3. Pair up with someone who chose the same picture you did. Tell your partner what you plan to say, discuss any changes or additions to your description and, together, write a caption for the picture.

Step 4. Get together with others who wrote a caption for the same picture and compare the similarities and differences in your work. Choose a caption you all like best.

Step 5. Get together with partners who prepared descriptions and wrote captions for the other pictures. Listen to and talk about each other's descriptions and captions.

Illustration One

Illustration Two

Preparing to Listen   77

Illustration Three

_____
_____
_____

Illustration Four

_____
_____
_____

Photos courtesy of Leader Dogs for the Blind, Rochester Hills, MI

ACTIVITY TWO   Reading Retell; Fact Gathering for Discussion

The training school you will hear about in this program is a large operation sponsored by the Lions Club, a nonprofit community organization active in many U.S. cities and towns. Gathering some preliminary facts about the school will provide you with some information to help you think about the topic and discuss it with others.

Part One: Reading Retell; Fact Gathering

Step 1. Choose one of the two texts (Text A or Text B) to scan quickly for information to complete the following chart.

Step 2 (Optional). Discuss the information you found with a partner who scanned the **same** text.

Step 3. Share information with someone who scanned a **different** text and complete the chart.

LEADER DOG SCHOOL FOR THE BLIND/INFORMATION CHART

What is the origin of the program (who, when, where)?	
What is the purpose of the school?	
Who can get a dog? At what cost?	

LEADER DOG SCHOOL FOR THE BLIND/INFORMATION CHART

Question	Answer
Which organization runs the school?	
How many teams have graduated from the school?	
Where is the school located? What buildings make up the facility?	
Describe the living conditions and health services for the animals.	
How many people work at the school?	
How great is the need for this training service?	
What is the school's 1994 operating budget?	

Text A

Leader Dogs for the Blind
1039 South Rochester Road
P. O. Box 5000
Rochester Hills, Michigan 48307
Phone: (313) 651-9011

HISTORY

Without doubt, one of the most dramatic and best known service activities of Lions is the Leader Dog program. The Leader Dog School was founded in 1939 by three Lions who were unable to obtain Leader Dogs from any other source. Founders were S. A. Dodge, Donald P. Schuur and Charles A. Nuttig; all of whom later served as President of the Leader Dog organization. Conceived in a dream, Leader Dog has grown to be one of the largest and finest dog guide schools in the world.

The whole enterprise began, with more courage than anything else, when a few Lions from Detroit, Michigan, purchased an old farmhouse which still stands in the center of a complex now valued at over seven million dollars. The Leader Dog School in Rochester, Michigan, is adjacent to an estimated 45% of the nation's blind.

During its first years of operation, only a few people graduated. In fiscal year 1991, 303 Leader Dog teams graduated; 303 more blind people went out into the world able to live a life of their own, despite blindness. Over 9,000 Leader dogs have been trained since the founding of the school in 1939.

For 52 years Lions have invested hundreds of thousands of dollars in the Leader Dog School, and have made it their major project. Each year their contributions increase; over 1.7 million was contributed by Lions during the fiscal year 1991 which ended June 30, 1991.

The Leader Dog School offers its services through the Lions of all states. Lions have the privilege of offering Leader Dogs to all who are eligible. Lions help spread the word that blind people who want to be free and mobile can have a Leader Dog for the asking. Any Lions Club member can write in behalf of a blind candidate to obtain an application. Leader Dogs for the Blind will consider it a privilege and a pleasure to serve that person under the auspices of the Lions.
Courtesy of Leader Dogs for the Blind, Rochester Hills, MI.

Text B

Leader Dogs for the Blind
Rochester, Michigan

Located on 14 acres at the corner of Rochester Road (M-150) and Avon Road (23 Mile). The Leader Dog downtown Rochester training facility is located on Walnut between 3rd and 4th streets, Lot #90.

Dormitory: The School has facilities for housing twenty-eight people, four instructors and a housemother. There are three recreation rooms, two laundry rooms, two dining rooms, a kitchen and two conference rooms.

Kennels: The kennels are staffed by experienced instructors, a kennel manager and assistants. There are facilities for housing 300 large dogs in tile stalls with radiant heat and individual drinking fountains.

Veterinary Hospital: A hospital with complete facilities including X-ray equipment and pharmacy is located in the center of the large kennel building. Dogs are checked regularly by the staff veterinarian.

Garages: Garages house four training vans for transporting 160 dogs daily, three passenger vans, two passenger buses and a station wagon for transporting students enrolled at the Leader Dog School, plus grounds maintenance equipment.

Office: A staff of twelve coordinate the affairs of the Leader Dog School under the supervision of the President.

Downtown Training Center: The downtown building provides a very comfortable lounge for the students while they wait their turn for training. The bus and passenger vans are driven directly into the building where the students unload. On the other end of the building there are openings for the training vans used to transport the dogs to Rochester for training. Dogs are thereby kept out of the cold or hot weather.

Staff: The Leader Dog staff is composed of 78 employees (13 part-time), twenty-two of whom are instructors.

Need: To meet the increasing requests for Leader Dog training it has been necessary to continually add on and build new facilities. The program is available to some 40,000 men and women who lose their sight each year. Most of them desperately want to continue being active on the job and in the community. Leader Dogs for the Blind is one of the largest producing schools of its kind in the world. The operating budget for fiscal year 1994 is 4,134,480.00.
Courtesy of Leader Dogs for the Blind, Rochester Hills, MI.

Part Two: Discussion Questions

What do you think? Read and consider the following questions. Write your ideas in note form and discuss them with others.

1. How are dogs trained to work as leader dogs?

2. How are the people and dogs teamed?

3. What are the benefits to a blind person in having a leader dog?

4. Describe people's reaction to encountering a blind person with a leader dog (on the street, using public transportation, at school or work).

ACTIVITY THREE **Predictions; Bridge to Listening**

Part One: Predictions

Based on what you know about the subject so far, what information would you predict this program will tell you about the Leader Dog School for the Blind?

Write your ideas on the lines below. You can write your ideas in either words or phrases, in question or sentence form. Write any ideas you have. Don't worry about whether they are good or bad or whether they are correctly written.

1. _____
2. _____
3. _____
4. _____

Discuss your predictions. Later, you can check to see what you were able to predict accurately.

Part Two: Bridge to Listening

The purpose of the introduction is to prepare you for the information in the program. It will give you an overview or a taste of something interesting to come.

Step 1. Cue your tape to the introduction of the show, which begins, "Every year tens of thousands." Turn on your tape.

Step 2. Listen to the introduction, which ends, "Don Gonyea has our report," without stopping the tape. Think about the information as you listen. Stop the tape at the end of the introduction.

Step 3. Write two or three important ideas in note form. The first answer is given as an example.

1. 10s of th. people/lose sight
2.
3.

Discuss your ideas with a partner or check the answer key. Compare these ideas with the predictions you made before.

Listening to the Tape

The activities in this section will help you to practice your skills in understanding and using the information you hear. Concentrate on the task you have to accomplish and practice the skills (for example, note taking) needed to complete the task. Remember the strategies for coping with listening to radio reports listed on page 5:

- Focus on what you understand.
- Don't worry about information that goes by quickly.
- Share information and clarify what you're not sure of.

Note Taking

In many of the activities that follow you will be identifying the main ideas, supporting points, and details and often writing what you hear in note form. These activities will help you get more of the important information in your notes more quickly.

For a few tips about writing quick notes as you listen, read the information on page 6. For more complete information about improving your note-taking skills, refer to the Guide to Note Taking (Appendix 1, p. 93).

ACTIVITY FOUR — Listening for the Main Ideas

Step 1. Listen to the program "Top Dogs in Detroit: Eyes for the Unsighted" without stopping. Think about the information as you listen. Stop the tape at the end of the program. Write four or five main ideas that you heard in note form.

1.
2.
3.
4.
5.

Step 2. Discuss your ideas with a partner or check the answer key.

ACTIVITY FIVE — Writing Focused Notes

When you listen to a radio report, you hear a wonderful mix of voices and sounds. The information that you hear is a mixture of factual information blended with opinion and emotion. A radio report isn't always organized in the same logical pattern as a good academic lecture. It follows a pattern of describing or explaining the important ideas (main points and details) related to the topic from the reporter's point of view.

Your task is to listen and take notes so that you will be able to explain the supporting points and important details of this report to someone who has questions about the Leader Dog School for the Blind. The focused notes you write for the general questions will help you to discuss the details of what you heard with others.

DIRECTIONS To take focused notes follow these steps:

Step 1. Read the following general questions and think about the information you heard. What details relating to each question can you recall?

1. Who attends this school? What is its purpose?
2. What happens during the five-month training course?
3. What information is given about Hooch and his training session?
4. How are dogs paired with owners?
5. What is Lindsay's experience with Doogie?

Step 2. If possible, discuss these questions with others.

Step 3. Rewind to the beginning of the program. Start the tape. As you listen, write details in note form for each of the questions you have just read and discussed. If necessary, take notes on a separate sheet of paper.

Read the sample notes to see what kind of detail is important and how to write in note form. Try taking notes yourself as you listen to the tape. Compare what you have written to the sample notes provided. Your wording may not be the same, but the ideas should be.

1. Who attends this school? What is its purpose?

    -prestige school
    -LDSFB Rochester, north of Detroit
    -Students/Gol. Retrievers
        Ger. Shepherds
        Labs
        Mixed br.
        All— Tr. for blind

2. What happens during the five-month training course?

3. What information is given about Hooch and his training session?

4. How are dogs paired with owners?

5. What is Lindsay's experience with Doogie?

Step 4. Stop the tape at the end of the program. Read over your notes. If you have a partner, discuss what you heard and wrote. As you read or discuss, add information to your notes.

Step 5 (Optional). Listen another time to confirm and complete your notes. Read your notes and discuss again.

ACTIVITY SIX   Comprehension Questions

Answering these questions correctly is a check on the accuracy of your listening.

Step 1. Read the following questions and use your notes to answer as many questions as possible. Write the answers to these questions **in note form**.

1. Where is this school located? How well known is it?

2. What are these students being trained to do?

3. What will the dogs be taught during their first four months in the program?

4. As the dogs progress, where are they taken and what are they taught?

5. How old is Hooch? How old does he think he is?

6. Where is Jim going with Hooch? Why is this a good training location?

7. How long does each dog's training session last?

8. What factors determine the pairing of a dog with a person?

9. What information is needed to evaluate which dog should go with which person?

10. What kind of dog is Doogie?

11. How does Clyde describe the process of being paired up with a dog? What are the benefits to him of having a leader dog?

12. How much does it cost to train a leader dog? How are these costs paid?

13. How many dogs are paired with new partners every year?

Step 2. Discuss the information with others.

Step 3 (Optional). If you need to, listen to the program to find answers that you don't have or can't agree on. Stop the tape when you hear the information you are listening for and write your answer.

Language Close Up

In this section you can practice listening for specific language. The activities focus on different features, such as improving your awareness of grammatical form or improving your ability to hear key details. The activities will help you to be more aware of the different tones, colloquial expressions, and speaking styles people use when they talk. You can learn vocabulary through the practice of guessing meaning from context.

ACTIVITY SEVEN

Language Focus: Asking and Answering Questions

In this program the reporter asked trainer Jim Gardner about the training session he was planning with "Hooch." The purpose of this activity is to make you more aware of the form and content of questions. Your task is to write the question you hear the reporter ask. To accomplish this task, follow these steps:

Step 1. Read the answer and write the question that you think the reporter asked.

Step 2 (Optional). Compare your answer with a partner. What are the similarities or differences in what you wrote?

Step 3. Compare your questions to those on the tape. How similar or different are they?

The first question is provided for you to help you locate the relevant sections on your tape.

Cue your tape to the beginning of this section.

1. Q: "Who's that, Jim?,"

    A: "This is Hooch."

2. Q: _____

    A: "Hooch, Hooch ah, he thinks he's still a puppy. He doesn't realize how big he is."

3. Q: _____

    A: "Gimme a paw. Ah, Hooch is about sixteen months."
    "Okay."
    "Yeah, he thinks he's about six months."

4. Q: _____

    A: "We're going to Royal Oak."

5. Q: _____

    A: "Well, there's a college there at Royal Oak and we'd like to try to get the dogs in the college because there's a variety of different floors, ah, hard, shiny, ah, tile, ah, linoleum, carpeting, steps, open stairways, lots of people, so we'd like to see how they react around that."

6. Q: _____

    A: "Well, for each dog it varies, but we're going to take probably about four dogs each, so we'll probably work with each dog approximately thirty minutes."

Check your questions with the transcript.

ACTIVITY EIGHT Vocabulary: Guessing Meaning from Context

You have heard the words **in bold print** in the program. In this activity you will focus on the language used and guess the meaning of these words from the context in which they are used.

Step 1. Read each sentence. Based on your understanding of the sentence, try to guess what the word or words mean.

Step 2. Write your own definition for the words in bold print. You can check your definition with a partner or consult your dictionary.

1. She went to a **prestigious** university—world renowned for its excellent teaching.

    Definition: _____

2. They looked at the different kinds of chocolate and couldn't decide which they wanted, so they ordered an **assortment** in order to try them all.

    Definition: _____

3. The brown dog with white spots was a **mixed breed,** not a purebred.

    Definition: _____

4. You have to follow his orders exactly; he demands total **obedience.**

    Definition: _____

5. She was a cheery person, usually smiling and happy; everyone remarked on her sunny **disposition.**

    Definition: _____

6. She couldn't tell me exactly how long the meeting would last; she thought she'd be finished at **approximately** 4:00 P.M.

    Definition: _____

7. From the beginning, their friendship was very strong and satisfying because their interests and personalities were so similar; everyone said that they were a **perfect match.**

    Definition: _____

8. She had to **navigate** the obstacle course on the ski hill and found it difficult to swerve around the posts as she came down the hill.

    Definition: _____

9. She didn't know if she was strong enough to complete the course; the training was much more **rigorous** than she had imagined.

    Definition: _____

10. Although they told him his **mobility** would be much less than before, he was able to move around a lot more than he had expected.

    Definition: _____

Follow-Up

The activities in this section will give you a chance to find out more about the topic of this unit and conduct some investigations of your own. You can work on some or all or just one of these activities. There are activities that you can work on alone or with others. You can adapt these activities to meet your needs; you may even think of projects of your own to undertake.

When you study language you often learn about things in life you never knew before.

Photos courtesy of Leader Dogs for the Blind, Rochester Hills, MI.

ACTIVITY NINE   **Scanning for Information from a Pamphlet; Reading Retells**

Pamphlets published by the Leader Dog School for the Blind describe the work of the school, as well as general issues related to the unsighted. These brochures instruct the public about how to act when encountering a leader dog and explain how important it is for blind people to be able to travel freely. What specific information is provided in these brochures?

Step 1. Read the list of questions to answer. Discuss what you think the answer might be with a partner.

Step 2. Scan (read quickly for key words and important ideas) one of the two texts.

Step 3. Look for the answers to as many of the following questions as you can:

1. How does a person using a leader dog want to be treated?

2. If you see a blind person with a dog, what things should you **not** do?

3. How should you approach a blind person to see if they need help?

4. How will a blind person respond to you if he or she needs help?

5. If a blind person asks for directions, how should you instruct them?

6. Should you ever pet a leader dog or give it food?

7. What should you know about how to approach or offer attention to a blind person?

8. What is one of the most important accomplishments for a blind person?

9. In what area of opportunity have blind people been able to gain increased access? How have these advances been made possible?

10. When did the leader dog movement begin? To whom has it been made available?

11. How large is the Leader Dog School's training program?

12. Describe the kinds of people who come to the Leader School to pair up with a canine partner.

13. What does the program do to meet the unique needs of individual blind people?

14. Why are mobility and the ability to travel important for a blind person?

Step 4. Share your information with someone who read the **same** text.

Step 5. Exchange information with a partner who read a **different** text. Complete the answers for all questions.

Brochure A: Free to Travel

It may be that when serious study is made of what was accomplished by visually impaired people of the 20th century, the ability to travel freely will be placed near the top of the list in importance. Progress made by the visually impaired can be measured in terms of the freedom they enjoy to live the same lives as their brothers and sisters live.

There have been other fields in which increased access has taken place. Visually impaired people have an increasing choice of jobs open to them. The old traditional occupations of manufacturing brooms and mattresses, caning chairs and tuning pianos, have all but disappeared. Computer technology has opened up new career opportunities and made it possible for the visually impaired worker to compete with their sighted counter parts. This represents a step forward toward better access.

The Leader Dog movement, which began in 1939, has changed the lives of thousands of blind men and women, throughout the United States and Canada and other countries as well.

Leader Dogs for the Blind has one of the largest training departments in the country. From a few part time instructors in the beginning, Leader Dogs has expanded to 20 full time instructors as well as a certified Orientation and Mobility Specialist. Leader Dogs will continue to respond to the growing demand for dog guides and independence.

Working with the assistance of other members of the staff, they are helping many students acquire a freedom of movement that will enable them to travel between home and work and participate in the social life of their community. Today, Leader Dog training is offered to almost all who can benefit by it.

Admittedly, the possessor of a well trained Leader Dog cannot travel as easily or as quickly as a sighted person, nor is his travel as independent as it would be if he or she could see. However, the amount of freedom acquired is perhaps the most highly prized achievement of large members of today's visually impaired men and women.

In its early stages the training program at Leader Dog dealt primarily with people from Michigan. Over the years it evolved into a much more comprehensive, far reaching program. The program has been designed to train the student just out of High School as well as people 70 years old and older.

Staff capabilities in Orientation and Mobility cover: body image, posture, gait, coordination, position and awareness of location. The entire program attempts to look at each person as an individual, assess the impairment and plan programs to insure effective and efficient travel.

To function within society comfortably, mobility is obviously the key. One does not necessarily have to travel in congested areas to be considered independent; yet, to be independent one must be able to travel.

Courtesy of Leader Dogs for the Blind, Rochester, MI.

Brochure B: When You Meet a Leader Dog

A Leader dog brings the visually impaired traveler, a great sense of independence. More and more blind people are trained with well disciplined and dedicated Leader Dogs each year. It is very important that all sighted people know something about the way a Leader Dog team works together. We should know how to act when we encounter a blind person and the Leader Dog. The team knows what to do—but do we?

A person using a Leader Dog wants to be treated like an independent person. So assume he or she is independent. If the person is in some sort of trouble, he or she will ask for help. Never rush up and startle a blind person by grabbing their arm. Simply ask, "May I help you?" If the blind person appears to be in need of some assistance—approach him or her on the right side. The Leader Dog will usually be on the left. Do not touch or take the blind person by the arm without first asking, if you can assist. Under no circumstances, should a person take hold of the Leader Dog or the harness, this will confuse the dog and startle the individual.

If a blind person does welcome your help, offer your left elbow. He or she will take it and drop the harness handle as a signal to the dog that the dog is "off-duty" temporarily. They may also instruct the dog to follow you. If the blind handler is seeking assistance for a street crossing, always take them all the way across the street and up on the opposite curb, where the dog will again resume its duties.

When traveling in an unfamiliar environment the Leader Dog traveler may seek directions just as a sighted person might. Speak directly to the person and not the dog. Do not call out the dogs name or try to get it to follow you. Give specific directions as to where to make turns so that the person can give the appropriate directional commands to the dog. In some cases the person may instruct the dog to "follow".

Do not pet a Leader Dog when it is in harness or when working. There is a natural impulse to pet a Leader Dog. They are friendly animals that like to be petted and allowed to romp and play, but the owner should always be consulted first. Always ask the owner's permission before touching a Leader Dog.

Do the blind diner a favor and DO NOT offer tasty morsels to the Leader Dog. The owner looks after the Leader Dog's diet very carefully—the animal is well fed and does his job most efficiently when a recommended diet is followed.

Remember that while a blind person appreciates attention the way we all do, he or she wants their friends, and other they meet, to be natural with them and not overly solicitous. A person enjoys independence because of the faithful Leader Dog. A person with a Leader Dog likes to get around on his own and really does not appreciate attention they don't need.

Pity should have no place in your approach to the man or woman who travels with a Leader Dog, for here is a person to be admired and respected for the victory he or she has won.

Courtesy of Leader Dogs for the Blind, Rochester, MI.

Check your answers with the answer key.

> **SUGGESTIONS FOR OTHER FOLLOW-UP ACTIVITIES**
>
> **Speaking:** Group Activities
> - Role-play/problem-solving task:
>   Matching Dogs with Their Owners
>   It will take a bit of research to learn the characteristics of different breeds.
>
> **Individual Activities**
> - Three-minute talk:
>   Prepare a talk that focuses on technological breakthroughs that make independent living possible for persons with physical disabilities. You may tape or orally present your talk.
>
> **Listening:** Individual/Group Activities
> - Guest speaker from local disabled persons' advocacy association
> - Using your skills at home:
>   Listen to a health broadcast related to the topic of this program—living with physical disabilities—or a show about some other health topic. Choose a TV or radio news show or documentary report. See pages 18–19 for details about this activity.
> - Movie:
>   View *A Brief History of Time*.

ACTIVITY TEN Self-Evaluation

Now that you have reached the final activity of this edition of *RadioWaves*, complete the following self-evaluation of the improvement in your listening skills.

For each of the following categories mark one of the following:

        Much improvement   (1)

        Some improvement   (2)

        More improvement needed   (3)

Hopefully, you feel that you have made some progress. With the listening skills you have improved, you should be able to understand, enjoy, and use information in listening tasks you undertake in the future.

( ) A. Listening for the over-all organization of information that you hear _____

( ) B. Understanding important ideas _____

( ) C. Understanding details _____

( ) D. Ability to take notes about information you listen to _____

( ) E. Ability to make good guesses about the information you hear _____

( ) F. Taking advantage of opportunities to ask questions and share information in English _____

( ) G. Feeling comfortable when listening to English-language media _____

( ) H. Having confidence to seek out opportunities for practicing your English _____

( ) I. Understanding current topics _____

( ) J. Ability to use the information you hear _____

APPENDIX 1
Guide to Note Taking

Note taking is a useful multi-purpose skill. There are many situations, whether listening or reading, in which you will want to remember information to use later. Having good note-taking skills will enable you to record the information you need. Note taking is also a useful tool to help you increase your comprehension and to extend your ability to use information as you learn English.

This program offers numerous opportunities to develop your listening comprehension as you develop your note-taking skills. In each edition of *RadioWaves*, there are programs on a variety of topics. As you listen, you will notice that the information is told in different ways. There are two approaches to note taking for information you listen to and use in speaking, reading, and writing activities.

Academic Note Taking

The first approach is the academic note-taking format that most university students and many professionals are familiar with. This format is used extensively in postsecondary education and in professional work. The academic note-taking format is useful for information that follows a logical pattern of presentation of a main idea, followed by explanation of this idea by means of a number of supporting points, each of which is explained in some detail. Once the information related to the first main idea is explained, a new main idea follows and is also explained by supporting points and details. The organization for these notes looks like this:

A. Main Idea
    1. Supporting Point
        a. Detail One
        b. Detail Two
        c. Detail Three
    2. Supporting Point

B. Main Idea

This note-taking format is used for those radio programs in which the information generally follows this pattern of development.

Focused Notes

The second format introduced and practiced in the *RadioWaves* note-taking activities is the use of focused notes. Taking focused notes consists of recording important points and details relating to a general question or issue explained at length in a radio show. Radio programs develop ideas through the exposition of facts presented by the reporter in combination with interviews that emphasize, reiterate, or elaborate those facts. They often use a journalistic style that blends fact with opinion, emotion, or personal impressions. This type of information may not follow a logical development. Occasionally, you will find that the information digresses from the point being explained. Using general questions as a way to help you focus on finding the important ideas and details is a useful method to help you hear when and how new information is introduced. It also helps you **not** to focus on unimportant information or side issues. Some possible formats for taking these notes follow:

Explanation

Question: What do doctors and nurses learn at the Hole in the Wall Gang Camp?

1. Supporting point
   a. Detail One
   b. Detail Two
   c. Detail Three
2. Supporting point
   a. Detail One
   b. Detail Two
   c. Detail Three

Narrative Points

Question	Supporting Points & Details
How can you describe Pia and the disease she has? How does it affect her?	(key ideas listed as separate points)

As you become more practiced at note taking for a radio magazine format and acquire better skills, you will recognize the introduction of a new idea more quickly and will be able to grasp more of the important points and details that are given.

Strategies

Whether using an academic or a focused note format, there are a number of strategies that are useful in getting more information in your notes. You can practice using these strategies as you complete the note-taking activities featured in each program. In general, these strategies include the following:

1. Writing key words only
2. Using abbreviations
3. Using symbols to represent certain words
4. Using spacing to show the relationship of ideas to each other
5. Paraphrasing (writing ideas in your own words)

Writing Key Words Only

Some words are more important than others; these are the words that carry the most meaning. Because of the way English is structured these words are usually the subject, the verb, and the object of the sentence. Words like adjectives, adverbs, prepositions, articles, and auxiliary verbs are more likely to be connecting the important words to each other in the sentence. For example, when you write a telegram you write only the essential content words. Most often, when you take notes it is not necessary to write the function words. Not writing these words leaves you more time to record a greater amount of important information. Look at the example taken from one of the programs in this edition. The important words are in bold print. Notice what part of speech this word is; subject, verb, object, or adjective. Notice what words are not important to write.

Example from "Butting Out in the Board Room"

THE **WARNER CABLE COMPANY** OFFICE IN **MILWAUKEE, WISCONSIN**, IS JUST ONE OF A **GROWING NUMBER** OF **BUSINESSES** IN THE **UNITED STATES ADOPTING NO-SMOKING POLICIES.** IN LIGHT OF **RECENT HEALTH STUDIES LINK**ING **SECOND-HAND SMOKE TO** LUNG **CANCER, COMPANY OFFICIALS** SAY THEY **DON'T** WANT TO UNNECESSARILY **JEOPARDIZE** THE **HEALTH** OF THEIR **EMPLOYEES.**

Key Words	Function Words
Warner Cable Co.	The, office in
Milwaukee, Wisconsin	is just one of a
growing number, businesses	of, in the
United States	in light of
adopting	say they
no-smoking policies	want to unnecessarily
recent studies	the
link second-hand smoke to cancer	of their
company officials	
don't	
jeopardize	
health	
employees	

Using Abbreviations

Abbreviations are shortened forms of words. There are standard abbreviations, which are universally recognized, for some words. Dictionaries include lists of standard abbreviations. Examples of these include the following:

A. Places:
   Countries: USA (United States of America)
           Fr. (France)
           Ch. (China)

States: MA (Massachusetts)
NY (New York)

Cities: Bos. (Boston)
NYC (New York City)

B. Titles:
Mr. (Mister)
M. (Miss)
Dr. (Doctor)
MD (medical doctor)
Pres. (President)
Co. (Company)

C. Dates:
Jan. (January)
Feb. (February)
Mon. (Monday)
Tues. (Tuesday)

D. Common Words:
neg. (negative)
pos. (positive)
ex. or e.g. (example)
N.B. (important information, don't forget)

E. Word Roots, Prefixes, and Suffixes
English words are sometimes composed of parts that have their origin in other languages. These parts have special meanings of their own.

Examples:

Word Part	Meaning
ante	before
bi	two
bio	life
non	not
ob	in the way
post	after
pre	before
psych	mind

Study guides often include lists of common English roots, prefixes, and suffixes.

In addition to using standard abbreviations, you can use your own abbreviations for note taking. This is useful when words that do not have a standard abbreviation are used repeatedly in a program. An example of this is using the first letter of a proper name to stand for the whole name. Often the first three or four letters of a word can be used to abbreviate it. When you use your own abbreviations, be sure to write the word **completely** the first time, with the abbreviation in brackets beside it, so that you will not forget the meaning of the abbreviation.

Example from "Butting Out in the Board Room"

THE WARNER CABLE COMPANY OFFICE IN MILWAUKEE, WISCONSIN, IS JUST ONE OF A GROWING NUMBER OF BUSINESSES IN THE UNITED STATES ADOPTING NO-SMOKING POLICIES. IN LIGHT OF RECENT HEALTH STUDIES LINKING SECOND-HAND SMOKE TO LUNG CANCER, COMPANY OFFICIALS SAY THEY DON'T WANT TO UNNECESSARILY JEOPARDIZE THE HEALTH OF THEIR EMPLOYEES.

Notes:
    No-Smoking Policy
        Warner Cable Co (W.C. Co.), Mi. Wl./
        Ex. no. of US business
        Why: Studies
            Show: 2nd.hand smoke → cancer
            Co. officials "no jeopardize wrkers health"

Using Symbols

You can use symbols to replace words. The use of such symbols as the numerical form of numbers or values in mathematical expressions is common in disciplines where calculations are frequently made.

Some examples of commonly understood symbols include the following:

Symbol	Meaning
=	the same as or equal to
≠	not the same
#	number
$	money
@	at
/ *	important detail
%	percentage
c	about
&	and
↑	increase
↓	decrease
→	result, direction (causal link)
∴	therefore

Using Spacing

In order to understand your notes, it is important to organize the way you write the information on the page. If you cannot read your notes later, you won't be able to use them. Use the space on the page to organize your notes.

You can divide your page and draw a line from top to bottom with a wide margin on the left to mark the main ideas.

Divided-Page Notes

Main Ideas	**Supporting Pts./Details**

When using a divided-page note format it is useful to write each separate point on a separate line and use indenting to show the relationship of ideas to each other. The following is an example (from "Butting Out in the Board Room") of a divided-page format:

Main Ideas	**Supporting Pts./Details**

B. "Coping without smoking" program	2. New Program
	   a. 1st/its kind in US
	   b. Used to help workers Cos. ban smoking
	3. Purpose:
	   a. distract smkers.

You can also use a tree-branching diagram format in which the tree anatomy of main trunk, limbs, and branches is used to show the different levels of main ideas, supporting points, and details. A tree diagram of notes looks like this:

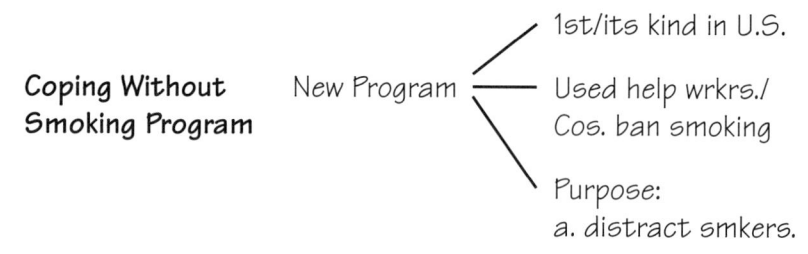

Coping Without Smoking Program — New Program
- 1st/its kind in U.S.
- Used help wrkrs./ Cos. ban smoking
- Purpose:
  a. distract smkers.

It is also possible to use a combination of these two in, for example, the use of branching details in a divided-page format.

Main Ideas	**Supporting Pts./Details**
B. "Coping Without Smoking" Program	

2. New Program
   - a. 1st/its kind in US
   - b. Used to help workers/ Cos. ban smoking

3. Purpose:
   - a. distract smkers.

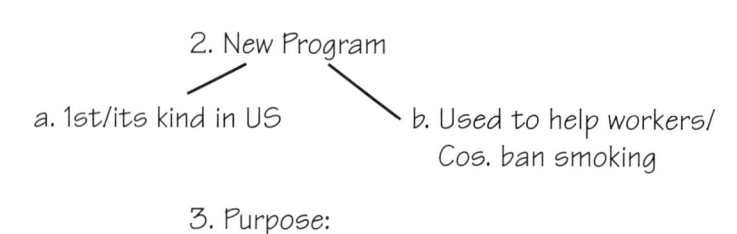

Another important aspect of spacing is the use of indenting and connecting lines, brackets, or diagrams. These show a relationship between or among ideas. Indenting or putting brackets around information shows that there is a link between these ideas. You can also use connecting lines or numbers to show a relationship among ideas.

    C. Marsh Electronics
        1.

        2. Results
          20 people
            5: quit
            rest: severe lmt. smoking

The points above will help you to write organized notes, but they are not the only ways to write what you hear. Everyone develops his or her own style of note taking. The goal is to have an organized system so that the information will be easy to read, understand, and use.

Paraphrasing

As you write notes while listening to the information in these programs, you will find it is impossible to write all of the important or key words you hear. Sometimes the information comes too quickly. Paraphrasing allows you to record the ideas without having to write all the words. It is possible to use simpler or fewer words to express the same idea as a longer or more complex group of words. This is a strategy that takes practice, and it becomes easier to use as your competence in English improves. As your language develops, it will become easier to paraphrase. Use paraphrasing whenever you can.

Example

"YOU MIGHT HAVE TO PHYSICALLY STEP OUTSIDE FOR A FEW MINUTES AND GET SOME FRESH AIR. DON'T . . . DON'T FORGET TO DO THAT. THAT . . . THAT DOES HELP A LOT OF PEOPLE."

Paraphrase:

    get outside/fresh air
    remember/

Note taking is done for a purpose. These strategies will help you to record a large amount of the information you hear so that you can use it later. Your comprehension of English increases as your ability to record information grows. This is a skill for language learning, but it is also a skill for life.

APPENDIX 2
Reporters' Biographies and Transcripts

Meet the People Behind the RadioWaves Health Edition

Karl Signell ("Medical Emergency 911") is a journalist from Hyattsville, Maryland. For him, "an audio documentary is like music." Signell's search for perfect sound has led him to digital recording and mastering for his documentaries. He is the producer of *Music in a New World: America's Ethnic Traditions* and the award-winning National Public Radio series "The Nature of Music."

Doug Gavel ("Butting Out in the Boardroom") is a frequent contributor to a variety of broadcast networks including CBS and ABC. His career in broadcasting has taken him from San Francisco, California, halfway across America to Milwaukee, Wisconsin, where he now lives and works. Gavel has won four Associated Press awards for sports broadcasting, and awards from the Associated Press for Best News Series 1989, and for Best Investigative Report 1992.

Phyllis Joffe ("Summer Camp for Sick Kids") is a print journalist and an independent radio and television producer based in New Britain, Connecticut. Joffe specializes in coverage of the arts, with special attention to issues of cultural diversity, human rights, and education. She is currently associated with Connecticut Public Radio and is a regular contributor to National Public Radio. Her radio features have also aired in Australia and Canada.

Stephanie O'Neill ("Tiny Survivors: Saving Preemies") began her multifaceted journalism career at age 17 as the youngest staff reporter ever at the *Contra Costa Times* newspaper near San Francisco. Later she switched to television news writing and then back to print as a reporter for the *Los Angeles Times*. A job as an on-air reporter/producer with California's public radio news network took her all over the state . . . and to San Francisco the night a huge earthquake rocked the city. O'Neill now works as a freelance journalist contributing to the *Los Angeles Times* and National Public Radio.

Don Gonyea ("Top Dogs in Detroit") is an award-winning journalist who covers the American automobile industry from Detroit, Michigan. He also files stories on everything from politics to poetry for National Public Radio. In addition to his radio work, Gonyea is a documentary film maker and teaches journalism at Wayne State University.

HEALTH

This program is brought to you by Heinle & Heinle Publishers in Boston, Massachusetts.

Welcome to *RadioWaves*. I'm Judith Ritter, and this is the Health Edition. In the area of health care, North Americans face enormous challenges in the nineties. Shrinking budgets and rising costs have put a strain on the system and on the individuals who use it. Most of what we hear is about dollars and cents, but on *RadioWaves* we look at the human side of health care. In this edition, "A Summer Camp for Sick Kids."

"They put a life jacket around me, and I got in. I did a bit of splashing. And I just knew I was swimming. That's when I realized . . . like . . . Hey! This is not a normal camp."

"Small Survivors: Saving Tiny Babies."

"I don't feel that he's lagged behind in anything because he's been premature, and he's just so smart."

"Butting Out in the Boardroom," and, in just a minute, "A Matter of Life and Death: Emergency Medical Services."

MEDICAL EMERGENCY 911

Maryland may be a small state, but it's a major player in developing medical emergency services. There are 49 hospitals that have 24-hour emergency departments. Nine of those hospitals are specially designated shock trauma centers, and there's a sophisticated communication center that links the state's ambulances, helicopters, and the hospitals. In Baltimore, Karl Signell takes us on a tour of Maryland's quick-response emergency system.

"A serious accident happens. Pre-hospital staff—paramedics, emergency medical technicians—through a sophisticated communication system know where and when the accident happened, and they are summoned immediately to provide the initial, quick, life-saving care."

That's Dr. Philip Militello. He's head of trauma surgery for the state system. If you have a serious injury anywhere in Maryland, this system will get you the right treatment with the least delay. What kind of help do you need? Where's the closest hospital? Should you go by ambulance or by helicopter? The answers to these questions come through sophisticated communications. The system springs into action with a telephone call to 911, your local emergency number anywhere in the state.

"Fire and rescue."

If you're injured, your call is forwarded to the fire department's emergency rescue service. Based on the information you give them, they send a radio call for the nearest available help.

"He has been shot. Hold on while I dispatch an ambulance."

A man has shot himself. The nearest available shock trauma ambulance is twenty minutes away. But a paramedic supervisor with some emergency medical equipment in his car responds to the radio call and arrives on the scene within nine minutes. A man with a bullet hole in his stomach and a dazed look slumps in a chair. There's blood on the floor. Police and fire rescue personnel swarm over the scene in contact with headquarters by radio and telephone. The supervisor, Lieutenant Mike Fahey, is a nationally certified paramedic. He quietly talks to the patient while he bandages the bullet hole. Finding the patient's blood pressure alarmingly low, he immediately starts intravenous blood plasma. His movements are deliberate and his voice is calm.

"Come in. Take control of the situation. Remain calm. Chaos is contagious, and so is the calm that you have. When the patient looks up at you and you're calm, then you're reassuring. Then they calm down."

The paramedic ambulance with advanced life support equipment arrives twelve minutes later, and Fahey's patient is loaded on a stretcher, ready to go. But the patient is in shock. If he stays in shock, he has a poor chance of survival. Inside the ambulance, they start another line of plasma and apply medical anti-shock trousers. Those are rubberized trousers to squeeze the blood from the legs back to the brain and other vital organs. Through radio communication everyone has agreed to send him by ambulance to the regional shock trauma center. It's only six minutes by land; it's available; and the regional center is equipped for his particular injury.

"They're putting on the trousers now. As soon as they get that, they'll be able to start going down the highway."

"If we can get the patient to the trauma center within twenty minutes, we go by land. If it's going to be longer than twenty minutes, we try to go by air."

Captain Linda Sterling. She's Mike Fahey's boss at the local emergency medical service. When one of her paramedics needs a med-evac helicopter, the request goes quickly to the SYSCOM, the statewide System Communication Center. Three large screens dominate the darkened room at SYSCOM. The right screen shows which hospital can take what kind of injury. The center screen shows the location of all med-evac helicopters. And the one on the left shows the helicopter landing pad at the main shock trauma center. SYSCOM operations chief Andy Polavski tells us what's happening.

"Part of the operation here is the SYSCOM operation: systems communications. They serve as the coordinators of the med-evac activity in the state. This is the dispatch point for the State Police helicopters and the U.S. Park Police helicopters."

SYSCOM can also connect by radio any paramedic in the state with any hospital or any emergency specialist. In shock trauma injuries, minutes can mean life or death. Maryland's communication system saves precious time by connecting citizens, ambulances, helicopters, and hospitals. Dr. R. Adams Cowley, founder of the system, said, "If I can get you and stop your bleeding and restore your blood pressure within an hour of your accident, then I can probably save your life." This is Karl Signell reporting from Trooper One helicopter base in Middle River, Maryland.

Coming up: "Butting Out in the Boardroom."

BUTTING OUT IN THE BOARDROOM

"Me and my Winston,
we got a real good thing,
a real good taste."

"Smoother, milder, tastier—Old Gold cigarettes."

For years, the tobacco companies spread their message loud and clear, and smoking was popular. But the tide began to turn in 1964 with the report from the top health official in the United States. The report linked cigarettes to lung cancer. Today, more than one in four people in the United States still smokes, but there are fewer and fewer places now to light up. Now even many workplaces are off-limits, leaving smokers craving and cranky. But in Milwaukee, Wisconsin, a few companies are sympathetic, and they're offering employees a course to quit. Doug Gavel is in Milwaukee, and he has this story on a new approach to an old habit.

"Did you want the basic cable, or did you want to go with . . ."

The Warner Cable Company office in Milwaukee, Wisconsin is just one of a growing number of businesses in the United States adopting no-smoking policies. In light of recent health studies linking second-hand smoke to lung cancer, company officials say they don't want to unnecessarily jeopardize the health of their employees. Deirdre Edwards is the human resources director for Warner.

"What really prompted the policy is the concern on our part, because of recent research findings, that second-hand smoke is very harmful to nonsmokers, who really aren't making the same decision as smokers to smoke. So we decided to make Warner Cable, here at the Milwaukee division, a safe and healthy work environment for everyone."

Warner's new policy bans all smoking inside the building.

"We're looking at 50 percent of our population having to acclimate themselves to this new policy—some very willing and others not so willing."

Some smokers at Warner, like Jenny Miller, tremble at the thought of eight hours without a cigarette.

"It's going to be hard at work, though, when it's a stressful situation. That's really hard. There's certain . . . um . . . something will happen . . . and I'll . . . I'll light up, and that's going to be really hard, I think."

But now there's hope for smokers like this one. Kathy Hoffman is with the American Lung Association of Wisconsin. She has developed a new program called "Coping Without Smoking." It's the first program of its kind in the country. It has been designed specifically to help out smokers who work for companies that ban smoking.

"Really what it amounts to is . . . you . . . you want to do anything and everything you can to distract yourself so you don't smoke."

"To get your mind off it."

"Right."

Hoffman conducts seminars like this one in business after business in Wisconsin, telling employees the steps they can take to adapt to the new nonsmoking policy. She urges them to take walks, nibble on carrot sticks, even tie rubber bands around their wrists—anything to get their mind off cigarettes.

"You might have to physically step outside for a few minutes and get some fresh air. Don't forget to do that. That does help a lot of people."

Hoffman usually speaks to small groups, but sometimes as many as 40 people will take part. Her seminars last about an hour and a half. They include two short videos and some written materials documenting the health risks of smoking and tips for kicking the habit. She says her program is low-key, and that's why it works.

"I think it's succeeding because of the nonthreatening, nonjudgmental approach that it has. We don't tell smokers when to quit, how to quit. We really enable them to do it on their own time frame. We just try to provide them with the tools to do that."

There's also plenty of lively discussion that leaves the smokers with a lot of things to do and think about.

"Some of the techniques to quit, like the rubber band around the wrist or, um, the cinnamon stick to chew on, things like that. And also, um, to stop and think why they're smoking . . . I think is a big thing too."

"What are the two or three keys for you?"

"The exercise, focusing on something else, and ah, just gearing my mind towards something positive. Every time I think, about 'I want a cigarette,' I think of something positive that I can get out of it."

Over at Marsh Electronics on the west side of Milwaukee, cigarettes are also off-limits. Employees now have to go to the break room if they want to smoke. Cathy Hoffman brought her seminar here last spring when the company implemented its no-smoking policy. Marsh executive, Bill Siox, says Hoffman's seminar was well worth the 300-dollar price tag.

"Of the twenty people who started the program, we have five who have quit. We have the rest of them . . . all of them . . . I . . . in fact . . . I talked with them this morning . . . all of them said that they have severely limited their smoking."

All told, Hoffman has taken her program to more than 80 companies in Wisconsin, and more are signing up every day. But Hoffman isn't stopping there.

"Where can you go from here?"

"Well, we are working right now with the program going national, and that's really been the push the last few months, and that's going real well. Certainly we'd love it to go internationally at some point."

Despite all the health studies, more than 46 million people in the United States still smoke, and more than 400,000 people die from smoking-related diseases every year. But little by little, crusaders in the war against smoking are making progress. Cathy Hoffman hopes her program is a valuable weapon in that fight for life. I'm Doug Gravel in Milwaukee, Wisconsin.

SUMMER CAMP FOR SICK KIDS

Every summer, thousands of American children congregate in New England where scores of overnight camps dot the rural landscape from Maine to Connecticut. The Hole in the Wall Gang Camp is one of those, and there, as at most camps, kids can swim, play soccer, do crafts, and put on plays. But at this camp, children are also learning to use poetry and other forms of creative writing to express feelings they've had to keep inside, feelings about being critically ill. Phyllis Joffe has a profile of one camper for whom the camp has made all the difference.

"We're going to have Pia read from part of her chapter. In it, she describes a dandelion."

It's a late summer afternoon at the Hole in the Wall Gang Camp in Ashford, Connecticut, a New England town about half an hour's drive from Connecticut's capital, Hartford. About half a dozen campers and counselors have gathered at the Hole in the Wall's gazebo by the pond for a creative writing workshop.

"That night Mona dreams of four bubbles. She can become a construction worker wearing a red hard hat, building trestles for the other flowers and ladders for ants, or an architect as rich as Dow Jones, with a pencil behind her left petal."

This may not seem like typical summer camp activity, but as 19-year-old Pia Taylor found out when she first arrived at Hole in the Wall, this is not a typical summer camp.

"I came here in '88. I wasn't all ecstatic about it. I just knew it was like some . . . they're just, they're just acting crazy, that's all. And I know it's going to be like Girl Scout or 4-H Camp, and I'm going to be stuck to the nurse's side or whatever . . . you know . . . just staying at the sidelines watching everybody play."

Pia Taylor is a husky young woman with a friendly smile and irresistible laugh. She walks with a limp. Pia has sickle-cell anemia, a crippling blood disease inherited mostly by people of African descent. Until Pia came to the Hole in the Wall Gang Camp, she had to avoid swimming pools because cool water made her body go into spasms of pain. But the Hole in the Wall Gang Camp is built for children who are sick. There Pia found a heated pool and sunlamps waiting to warm her when she got out of the water.

"They put a life jacket over . . . around me, and I got in. I did a bit of splashing, and I just knew I was swimming. You couldn't tell me anything when I was in that pool. I was having me some fun! And I was fine . . . and that's when I realized . . . like . . . Hey! This is not a normal camp . . . you know. They really went beyond the limits of the regular camp."

At this 300-acre, lakeside camp built on land that was once a farm, every building has ramps and special equipment for children who ride in wheelchairs or electric carts. The whole place looks like a set for a Hollywood western, like Paul Newman's movie "Butch Cassidy and the Sundance Kid." It's no coincidence. Newman started the camp in 1988. More than 3,000 youngsters have attended so far. The Hole in the Wall only admits seriously ill children. There are special sessions for HIV-positive kids and kids like Pia Taylor with sickle-cell disease.

"Three or four summers ago, we decided that, although our major mission is children with cancer . . . that there were a lot of kids with sickle-cell disease who really did not have the opportunity to go to camp in the summer."

Pediatrician Howard Pearson has been the camp's medical director since it opened. He teaches at Yale University and he's an expert on sickle-cell disease. But until he spent an entire week with a hundred sickle-cell kids at the Hole in the Wall Gang Camp, he says he didn't fully comprehend the disease's impact.

"Well at camp, unlike the hospital, if a child says he's hurting . . . or complaining . . . or that sort of thing . . . nurses and doctors working in the infirmary hear about it right away. And so we kept statistics of that seven-day experience for these hundred children, and what we found is that 50 percent of them . . . of those hundred children . . . in the seven-day period of time, had an episode of pain. That was far, far greater than I had ever realized, working in a hospital."

While the Hole in the Wall Gang Camp gives its staff—including two doctors, five nurses, thirty program directors, and thirty counselors—an unusual opportunity to observe the day-to-day rhythms of a sick child's life, it also gives the kids a rare chance to relax and just be themselves. Paul Newman started the camp as a place where, in his words, sick kids can go "raise a little hell." For camper Pia Taylor, that meant a place where she not only could finally splash around in the water without fear, but also where, in her creative writing workshop, she could communicate feelings she'd never talked about before.

"I don't want to rush anything. I just want to experience having my driver's license in my pocket, or college life. I want to take my SATs. I want to take a moment to look at the sky because if I don't, in a minute from now, I may not be able to see it."

Pia Taylor's essay, and the writings of six other children, appear in the book *I Will Sing Life: Voices from the Hole in the Wall Gang Camp,* published by Little, Brown. Meanwhile, Paul Newman hopes his Connecticut camp will be a model for others like it throughout the world, including one he's now building in Ireland. I'm Phyllis Joffe in Hartford, Connecticut.

And I'm Judith Ritter, and later on, "Top Dogs in Detroit: Training America's Lead Dogs." But just ahead, "Tiny Survivors."

TINY SURVIVORS: SAVING PREEMIES

Worldwide, a large number of babies are born prematurely. They're the infants who don't make it to the 37 to 40 weeks of a full-term pregnancy. In the United States, the pre-term delivery rate is about 7 percent. But now, new technological advances have greatly improved the chances of survival for these tiny infants, some of whom are born months before they're due. Stephanie O'Neill has that story from Los Angeles, California.

Like most expectant parents, Shirley Jordan and Jeff Shaefer were eagerly planning the arrival of their first child. But the Hollywood couple was taken by surprise when Shirley went into labor almost two months before her due date.

"We were sitting at my girlfriend's house, and we were planning our baby shower. And I felt something a little funny, but I wasn't quite sure because I was in my seventh month, or just getting into the seventh month, and I wasn't sure how I was supposed to feel at that point."

But it was happening and Shirley Jordan gave birth nearly two months early to a four-pound, three-ounce boy. But today's technology put his chance for survival high. In fact, little Jordan Shaefer, who is now a healthy, thriving toddler, was home with his parents just ten days after his premature birth. Dr. Myron Bethel is an obstetrician at the Hospital of the Good Samaritan in Los Angeles. He says, while there have been significant advances in keeping premature babies alive, there's been little progress in lowering the number of pre-term births.

"I don't think we've gotten any better at preventing pre-term labor, or actually even any better at identifying those patients who are at risk. We have the empirical, ah, information that we give them: to decrease the amount of work and occupational exposure to stress . . . increase in hydration . . . and relative rest is the only thing that we can offer."

The biggest killer of premature babies is underdeveloped lungs that aren't strong enough to support them. And that's where doctors like Ralph Franciskeeny come in. He's a neonatologist and a director of the premature baby intensive care unit, or PICU ward, at Kaiser Hospital in Hollywood. Inside the nursery, sophisticated machinery works full-time keeping alive more than a dozen tiny infants.

"This baby's in an incubator. It's a double-wall, plastic-shielded bed that blows warm air over the baby continuously. By doing that, we can maintain this baby's body temperature within a narrow range, so that the baby doesn't stress as a result of being cold."

The baby, who is five days old, is hooked up to one of the more recent technological breakthroughs, the so-called high-frequency ventilator, which vibrates air into his lungs at a rate of 600 to 1,000 pulses per minute. The new ventilator can better give oxygen and remove carbon monoxide from the infant's blood than traditional ventilators. But more importantly, it is far more gentle on his fragile lungs. Doctors have attached a small light sensor to this baby's foot to tell them how much oxygen his blood is absorbing.

"By doing that, we can fine-tune the amount of oxygen this baby gets . . . uh . . . without doing a lot of invasive laboratory work by sticking him and drawing blood gases."

"And can the parents touch the baby in this? Can they pick it up?"

"Yeah, the parents can, uh, you know, open the doors, touch the baby, and if the baby's not, uh, getting a whole lot of support, the parents can actually hold the baby."

Until recently, premature babies were at risk of developing fatal lung disease because their immature lungs lacked an essential substance called surfactant, which enables the lungs to expand and shrink with each breath. Now doctors have available a synthetic surfactant. Again, Dr. Ralph Franciskeeny:

"We can actually squirt that down in the lungs through an intratrachea tube that goes down in the lungs, and by doing so, accelerate, if you will, the baby's ability to breathe on his own, so that that infant really doesn't need a lot of ventilatory support after that."

If not for such breakthroughs, most of the babies in this nursery wouldn't have survived much past birth. Today, however, it's not uncommon for babies born at six months of gestation to make it home with their parents, and then quickly catch up with their peers. Shirley Jordan says she sees little difference between her son and other children his age.

"He's had no problems. He's grown up to be, as you can see, a very healthy young man. And he's just so smart . . . so smart. I don't feel that he's lagged behind in anything because he's been premature."

Still doctors in the neonatology field are continuing their efforts at improving the well-being of these tiny, fragile patients with the hope of saving even more premature babies. In Los Angeles, California, I'm Stephanie O'Neill reporting.

TOP DOGS IN DETROIT: EYES FOR THE UNSIGHTED

Every year, tens of thousands of men, women, and children lose their ability to see. But losing sight doesn't necessarily mean the person has to become dependent. In the classroom and at home and at work, braille type and talking computers have given the blind access to the written word. But an equally vital challenge to those who lose their sight is maintaining the ability to travel independently, and that's an area where a world-renowned school in Michigan has been excelling for more than five decades. Don Gonyea has our report.

Meet the student body of one of the most prestigious schools of its kind in the entire United States. As you've probably guessed, this is no ordinary school. It's the Leader Dog School for the Blind in Rochester, Michigan, located just north of Detroit. The students at this school are an assortment of golden retrievers, German shepherds, Labradors, as well as a wide variety of mixed-breed canines. All are being trained to work as a leader dog for someone who has lost their sight. Brad Scott is the school's director of training.

"There's a five-month cycle, basically. The first four months with the instructors training the dog. They start the dogs out in a very low-stress environment. They are dealing primarily with understanding the dog, getting to know the dog . . . work out some basic obedience . . . find out where his disposition is, his temperament, things of that nature. As the time goes on during that four-month cycle, they'll get involved with basic obedience, teach the dog: *sit, down, stay, heel, come* . . . "

And as the dog progresses, it is taken out to do some work on the streets of a nearby town or city. The dog is taught to stop at curbs, and how to make sure there is no traffic before crossing a street, and—perhaps most important of all—to resist the urge to chase a squirrel. Trainer Jim Gardner is preparing for a trip out on the town with four dogs he is currently working with.

"Who's that, Jim?"

"This is Hooch."

"What can you tell me about Hooch?"

"Hooch . . . Hooch . . . he thinks he's still a puppy. He doesn't realize how big he is."

"How big is he, and how old is he?"

"Give me a paw. Hooch is about 16 months. Yeah. He thinks he's about six months."

"Where are you guys heading today?"

"We're going to Royal Oak."

"And what are you going to do there with Hooch?"

"Well, there's a college there at Royal Oak, and we like to try to get the dogs in the college because they've got a variety of different floors: hard, shiny, tile, linoleum, carpeting, steps, open stairways, lots of people. So we like to see how they react around that."

"And how long will the training session last?"

"Well, for each dog it varies, but we're going to take probably about four dogs each, so we'll probably work with each dog for approximately 30 minutes."

Then, at the end of four months of work with trainers like Jim Gardner, comes the time when the dogs are introduced to their new owners. The school's Brad Scott says a lot of thought goes into deciding which dog will be paired up with which person. There must be a perfect match, he says, of personalities between canine and human. Certain dogs, says Scott, are better for certain things.

"We issue the dogs to these people after three days of evaluating what is the best dog for that person. We have to know where they live, what they do, what kind of travel they have. It makes a difference as to whether or not somebody is a judge or a student who spends many hours sitting quietly and still, or somebody who is very athletic and does many hours of walking. A wide variety of lifestyles out there and a wide variety of dogs . . . and we need to pick the right dog. That's the most important part of the process—is picking the right dog for the student."

"Doogie, sit. Down. Good girl."

"Tell me a little about Doogie."

"Doogie's a Doberman pinscher mixed with Lab. She's twenty months old, black, and a female."

35-year-old Clyde Lindsay was just paired up with Doogie two weeks ago. He says having a leader dog is a step up from using a white cane to navigate. According to Lindsay, working with a leader dog is like developing a friendship.

"It's, uh, you know, getting to know each other, getting to accept each other, uh, good communication with the dog, and the dog being able to communicate with me."

Lindsay lost his sight as a result of glaucoma 13 years ago. Doogie is his second leader dog. He calls her his partner.

"I can travel more freely, more independently, you know . . . lot of times, when there's just a cane—I have another pair of eyes watching out for me."

And Lindsay says, when he and Doogie go out walking, he is trusting her with his life. It costs about $11,000 to put a dog through the rigorous training it gets at the Leader Dog School for the Blind, but the cost to the person actually getting a dog is covered 100 percent through fund-raising the school does. People come from around the world to Michigan's Leader Dog School for the Blind. Thee hundred dogs are matched with new partners every year, putting those who can't see back on the road to greater mobility and independence. I'm Don Gonyea, in Detroit, Michigan.

And that's it for the Health edition of *RadioWaves*.

We welcome your comments and suggestions. So if you'd like to contact us, our address is *RadioWaves*, Heinle & Heinle Publishers, 20 Park Plaza, Boston, Massachusetts, USA, 02116. Or send us a fax at 617-426-4379.

RadioWaves is a production of Dana Knight Communications. Sylvain Gaspe is our production assistant. Our engineers are Normand Rodrigue and John Smith.

If you enjoyed this program, be sure you check out our other shows. *RadioWaves* brings you programs on sports, environment, business, entertainment, and music. I'm your host, Judith Ritter. Thanks for listening, and be sure to join us for another edition of *RadioWaves*. Bye for now.

RadioWaves is brought to you by Heinle & Heinle Publishers. Heinle & Heinle is committed to making language learning more effective, satisfying, and enjoyable for students and teachers.

APPENDIX 3

Answer Key

Medical Emergency 911

Activity Two

1. Call 911 for assistance
2. Pull ahead and completely off the road—Put on emergency flashers—Determine location using mile marker or exit sign—Get help by sending someone, using Channel 9 on CB radio, or using cellular phone—Give location, type, # of victims, and your name—Do not move patients unless danger of fire, explosion, or further injuries.
3. Pull over and stop as soon as possible to let it pass.
4. 50 hospitals with 24-hr. emergency care—10 trauma centers—1 shock trauma center for critical injuries and 20 specialty referral centers for special injuries (e.g., spinal cord, burns, etc.). Also network of ambulances and helicopters to transport patients to any of these centers.
5. As fast as 201 mph by helicopter if necessary.

Activity Three

1. B   2. D   3. A   4. E   5. C

Activity Four, Part Two

2. 49
3. 9
4. Links state's ambulances, helicopters, and hospitals

Activity Five

1. A   2. B   3. C   4. D

Activity Seven

2. By dialing 911
3. To fire dept. emergency rescue service; then call sent to nearest help, depending on information given
4. Shooting accident
5. Paramedic supervisor; 9 min.
6. Nationally certified paramedic; bandages bullet hole, starts intravenous plasma
7. Calmly; calms patient down
8. In shock
9. Start more plasma; apply medical anti-shock trousers to squeeze blood from legs back to brain and other organs
10. To send him by ambulance to regional shock trauma center; center is 6 min. away by land, available, and equipped for this type injury
11. If can reach trauma center in less than 20 min., go by land; otherwise, go by air

12. Statewide Systems Communication Center; 3 large screens that show: which hospitals take which type injury; location of helicopters, landing pad at main center
13. Dispatch point for State and U.S. Park Police helicopters
14. Connect them by radio to hospitals and emergency specialists
15. Stop bleeding and restore blood pressure within hour of accident

Activity Eight
1. Dr. Philip Militello, head of trauma surgery
2. Mike Fahey, paramedic supervisor
3. Linda Sterling, Mike Fahey's boss
4. Andy Polavski, SYSCOM operations chief

Activity Ten
1. Overburdened, understaffed, and underfinanced because of
   - 37 million patients with no health insurance.
   - Growing # of aging who need expensive treatment.
   - Insufficient gov't reimbursement.
   - AIDS epidemic and drug violence.
2. 90 million
3. Long working hours (12-hr. shifts) with no break
   - Extremely busy—average of 200 patients/shift
   - Patients lined up in waiting rooms, hallways, closets
4. Korea and Vietnam wars; saving lives depended as much on speed as skill.
5. Trauma leading cause of death for people under age 44—140,000 deaths/yr. in United States
6. In Peoria, traffic deaths dropped 50%; in Orange County, non–head-injury fatalities dropped from 73%–9%.
7. That most accident victims would be middle-class and well insured; in cities, most patients are not able to pay.
8. Tightened control over how much hospitals could charge Medicare patients—people released too soon, then come back, sometimes sicker.
9. To cut down on costs (ICU beds most expensive); burden other units, make patients wait to receive care.
10. Poor and underinsured who cannot visit doctor during working hours.
11. Think care is better and is open 24 hrs.
12. Have become the family doctor
13. Put more money into the system in order to:
    Provide universal access to affordable health care
    Pay nurses better
    Give doctors flexibility in treating patients
    Improve preventive care
    Ration health care (e.g., spend less money on terminally ill; discourage transplants for elderly patients)

Butting Out in the Board Room

Activity Two

1. 68%
2. Concerns about health; state or local laws
3. 49% of companies responding to a 1991 Bureau of National Affairs survey have received complaints; improve communication of policy to employees, add restrictions or more strictly enforce existing ones.
4. Morale declined for 27% of smokers; breaks longer or more frequent.
5. Help and encourage them: literature, programs, incentives
6. Yes: 16% plan to adopt policy, 44% considering policies.

Activity Three, Part Two

2. More than a quarter of nation's population; because today smoking prohibited many places.
3. Offering a course to help smokers quit.

Activity Four

1. No-smoking policy/Warner Cable Company
2. New program/Coping Without Smoking
3. No-smoking policy/Marsh Electronics

Activity Six

2. Health studies/harm to nonsmokers and they did *not* decide to smoke.
3. No smoking in building; 50%.
4. Worried because feels will *have* to smoke when under stress.
5. A new program; to help smokers in companies where smoking not allowed.
6. Ways to distract themselves from smoking: walks, nibbling carrots, tying rubber bands around wrist.
7. Two videos, written material/health risks, tips to help stop.
8. Low-key, i.e., nonthreatening, nonjudgmental.
9. Smoking only allowed in break room.
10. Pleased/well worth the money.
11. 5 out of 20 quit, and rest severely limited smoking.
12. 80; go national and then international.
13. More than 40 million smokers; more than 400,000 smoke-related deaths.
14. Help people fight smoking.

Activity Seven, Steps 2, 3, & 4

1. gonna . . . really hard ... something will . . . I'll, I'll, . . . gonna
    A. c
    B. Gonna—going to; I'll, I'll—I will
2. to quit . . . um . . . chew on, things . . . um, to . . . you're . . . is
    A. a.
    B. You're—you are; is—that is

Appendix 3   Answer Key   111

3. focusing...something else...uh...gearing...something positive...I wanna
   A. b.
   B. I wanna—I want to; think of—I think of

Activity Ten, Part Two
1. $22 billion
2. $43 billion
3. $18.5 billion
4. $4,600; $8,000–$10,000
5. Results showed smokers of one or more packs/day:
   - Filed 18% costlier medical claims.
   - Spent 25% more days in hospital.
   - Were 29% more likely to file claims exceeding $5,000.
6. Smoking not consistent with image of health care office; cost of smoking very high: $1,100/year/smoker.
7. Smoker misses 2.2 more days of work/year.
8. Decreases.
9. Computers very sensitive to smoke, subject to high risk of damage.
10. Separate ventilation systems to withdraw smoke-filled air.
11. Environmental tobacco smoke; lung cancer risk to nonsmokers.
12. Much cheaper to help smokers quit ($64–$200) than to pay subsequent medical costs (over $150,000).

Summer Camp for Sick Kids

Activity Three, Part Two
2. Swimming, playing soccer, doing crafts, and putting on plays.
3. Learning to use poetry and creative writing to express feelings kept inside about being seriously ill.

Activity Four
1. B   2. D   3. A   4. C

Activity Six
2. Thought would just sit beside nurse and watch everybody else play, like at previous camps.
3. Husky, friendly smile, irresistible laugh, has a limp.
4. Blood disease inherited mostly by people of African descent.
5. Cold water makes her body spasm in pain; heated pool, sunlamps waiting to warm her.
6. Enjoyed it, realized this camp different from others.
7. 300 acres, beside lake, originally a farm; ramps and equipment for children in wheelchairs or electric carts.
8. '88; 3,000.
9. Camp medical director; sickle-cell disease.

10. 50% of them experienced incidents of pain (much higher than he had realized).
11. Two doctors, five nurses, 30 program directors, and 30 counselors.
12. Able to communicate feelings never talked about before.
13. Hopes it will be model for others; building similar camp in Ireland.

Activity Nine
1. They appear normal.
2. For medical procedures necessary for the night (e.g., pump, pills, etc.).
3. Head nurse; decides who gets admitted.
4. Based on disease (e.g, can only accept certain # of hemophiliacs because labor-intensive).
5. At least once/10-day session; goes out through In Door so has to stand in middle of room and pantomime words of song.
6. Very little/none; to be hugged—camp experience intense.
7. Every child needs a good childhood to grow to adulthood.
8. Medical director.
9. That maybe their disease is not so bad.
10. 2/3; have had chemotherapy, surgery, and radiation.
11. Disease caused by blood that lacks clotting factor; received blood in the past not tested for HIV, so 50% are HIV+ve.
12. Quiet time before bed: counselors and campers talk by candlelight.
13. Meeting interesting people, going to Hole in the Wall Gang Camp.
14. Makes them tough, go through it because no choice.

Tiny Survivors: Saving Preemies

Activity Two
1. $5\,^3/_4$ lbs.
2. 7"
3. 5–20%; 90–95%
4. Fused shut; partly open, can follow objects; almost fully developed
5. Unable to regulate body temp., ward off infection; becomes smooth as layer of fat develops

Activity Three, Part Two
2. Pre-term delivery rate in United States about 7%
3. Now chance of survival greatly improved

Activity Four
1. D 2. B 3. C 4. A

Activity Six
2. 4 lbs., 3 oz.; healthy, thriving toddler.
3. Preventing premature births.
4. Underdeveloped lungs—not strong enough to support babies.

5. Intensive care unit with sophisticated machinery.
6. Bed with double wall, plastic shield, and hot air blowing continuously over baby; maintains body temp. within certain range so baby does not get too cold.
7. Ventilator that vibrates into lungs at rate 600–1,000 pulses/sec.
8. Gives oxygen to, removes carbon monoxide from, lungs.
9. Light sensor; tells how much oxygen lungs are absorbing; can control oxygen without having to take blood samples.
10. Yes; if baby not getting lot of support can hold it.
11. Enables lungs to expand and shrink with every breath; they do not produce it.
12. Have made synthetic surfactant that can be squirted into lungs through tube.
13. Allow many preemies to survive, even when born 6 months gestation.
14. Sees little difference between him and others of his age. Thinks he is very smart.
15. Want to try and save even more.

Activity Ten, Step 1

Theme: What is the state of neonatology today? The problems that babies and the parents of babies born prematurely face. The difficulties that doctors, nurses and society face in providing care to preemies. The current practice as well as future of neonatology. The triumphs enjoyed and the defeats suffered in trying to save the lives of premature babies.

Activity Ten, Step 2

A. Advances in Neonatology
B. Health problems of preemies at birth
C. Experiences of parents and their premature infants
D. Financial and care-giving problems parents of premature infants face
E. Ethical issues doctors and families must face
F. Care-giving and the routine of working in an ICN

Top Dogs in Detroit: Eyes for the Unsighted

Activity Two, Part One
- 3 Lions: Dodge, Schuur, Nutting; 1939; Detroit, Michigan
- To train leader dogs for blind people
- Anybody legally blind, in good health, over 18, out of school; no cost
- Lions
- More than 9,500
- Rochester, Michigan; dormitory, kennels, hospital, garage, office, downtown training center
- Tile stalls, radiant heat, individual drinking fountains; veterinarian, X-ray equipment, pharmacy
- 78
- Very high: 40,000 lose sight/year
- $4,134,484.00

Activity Three, Part Two

2. Braille and talking computers
3. School that enables blind to travel independently

Activity Four

1. Students at the school
2. The training program
3. Hooch and his training
4. Pairing dogs and owners
5. Lindsay and his dog Doogie

Activity Six

1. Rochester, Michigan; best in the United States
2. Work as leaders for blind
3. Basic obedience commands: sit, down, stay, heel, come
4. To street: to stop at curb, when to cross, not to chase squirrels, etc.
5. 16 months; 6 months
6. To a college. Variety of floors (e.g., hard, tile, linoleum, shiny, carpeting). Also stairways and lots of people; want to see how dogs will react
7. 30 min.
8. The personalities of dog and human
9. Where person lives, what he does, kind of travel; e.g., student who sits a lot vs. athletic person who moves a lot
10. Female Doberman pinscher mixed with Lab, black, 20 months old
11. Like friendship: have to get to know, accept, and communicate with each other. Can travel more freely and independently
12. $11,000; fund-raising
13. 300

Activity Nine

1. As independent person
2. Never rush up/startle/grab their arm
3. Ask "May I help you?"
4. Offer elbow/dog off-duty/may instruct dog to follow you
5. Give directions to person, **not** dog; owner gives dir.s to dog
6. Always ask before petting/no food
7. Be natural/not overly solicitous
8. Ability to travel freely
9. Choice of jobs/computer technology
10. 1939/Thous. people in U.S./Can./other countries
11. Largest in country/20 full-time instructors
12. High school to 70s and older
13. Assess impairment; plan program for effective, effic. travel
14. Ensure independence